FRAUD
The Growth Industry

Harry West

KOGAN
PAGE

BRITISH INSTITUTE OF MANAGEMENT

First published in 1987 by
Professional Publishing Limited,
7 Swallow Place, London W1R 8AB

First published in 1988 by
Kogan Page Ltd,
120 Pentonville Road, London N1 9JN
in association with
British Institute of Management,
Management House, Cottingham Road,
Corby, Northants NN17 1TT

British Library Cataloguing in Publication Data
West, Harry
    Fraud: the growth industry.
    1. Great Britain. Commercial fraud. Control.
    I. Title   II. British Institute of Management
    346.1′ 63

    ISBN 1-85091-621-7

Printed and bound in Great Britain by
Biddles Ltd, Guildford, Surrey.

My wife, like most policemen's wives, has been directly and indirectly involved with my work for many years. Had it not been for her support, love and help my task would have been that much harder. I dedicate this book to her as a token of my love and gratitude.

Contents

FOREWORD

by

THE LORD KNIGHTS CBE QPM CBIM DL
Chief Constable, West Midlands Police, 1975–85

One of the most worrying features of our post-war society has been the seemingly inexorable and phenomenal increase in recorded crime. During the past 25 years the annual total figure has increased from 806,900 in 1961 to 3,847,400 in 1986, an overall growth of 376 per cent.

Within these figures reported offences of fraud, that is to say the inducing of a person (or organisation) by deceit to act to his (or its) injury, increased by 210 per cent from 39,651 to 122,802. These comparisons, however, can be no more than illustrative, as recording bases change over the years and, more importantly, many offences regarded as falling within the colloquial term 'fraud' for statistical purposes are recorded under other headings such as 'theft by employees'.

Of even greater significance, however, is the fact the figures quoted relate solely to crimes which have been reported to the police and the extent of unreported offences is extremely difficult, if not impossible, to assess. It is particularly difficult so far as fraud is concerned as it differs from most other forms of crime in that by its very nature the victim rarely, if ever, appreciates that he has been deprived of his money or property until well after the event. When he does realise it, for various reasons he is often reluctant to inform the police. Indeed, in the field of computer crime it has been suggested that 70 per cent of revealed offences are not reported, and the number of unrevealed ones is anybody's guess.

As to the losses resulting from this form of crime, a survey of company fraud published in 1985 put the figure at £3 billion a year, with nearly half of Britain's companies having been victims. A later survey, sponsored by the Police Foundation, the Home Office and

Arthur Young, put the figure at about £1 billion, with the number of recorded offences increasing annually by five per cent. The CBI estimates computer crime alone to be running at an annual figure of £25 to £30 million.

Whatever the true figures may be it is clear that the fraudster has the potential to strike at the very roots of an individual's or company's solvency, and it is no exaggeration to say that fraud could undermine the whole basis of international financial arrangements if allowed to go unchecked. If this crime is to be contained, clearly the first objective must be to develop a much greater awareness of the damage which fraud can and does cause to businesses of all kinds. Events in the City in the last year or so have undoubtedly heightened the level of appreciation of the danger, and the recent decision of the Government to set up a national Serious Crime Office to investigate the really major offences has evidenced their intention to tackle the problem at a high level. Coupled with this must come also a greater readiness to report these matters when they are detected. Just as vital, however, is an increased realisation that, like all other crime, offences of fraud, even given the increased sophistication and greater opportunities brought about by the introduction of computer systems, *can* be reduced if sensible precautions are taken by those who are potentially at risk.

Who better to give advice on these matters than someone who has spent many years investigating such offences and identifying the loop-holes which the fraudster exploits? As a member, and later the officer in charge, of the West Midlands Police Commercial Branch, one of the largest in the country, Mr West had unrivalled opportunities to examine at first hand the methods adopted by such criminals, and the practical case studies which he outlines clearly demonstrate that often it is inattention, inefficiency and poor management on the part of the losers which provide the opportunity for the offenders to operate without detection. Much of this is probably already well-known to the large corporations although as the surveys and press reports regularly show they are still vulnerable, and this despite having accountants, corporate treasurers, auditors and audit committees to help them. Small businessess, however, so many of which are being set up today, generally do not have such experts available to them and I believe that for them this book will be particularly useful. The consequences of fraud in their case can be catastrophic but they will find here much valuable advice and information which will not only help their managers and directors to increase their knowledge and awareness of this particularly insidious form of crime but also to develop their defences against it.

I believe Mr West has made a very worthwhile contribution to the current campaign to control and reduce as far as possible the activities of those who seek to divert to their own pockets the fruits of others' hard work. I commend his book to anyone who is anxious to ensure so far as he can that any attack on his profits, whether from within or without his business, is, if not impossible, at least identified and dealt with before it becomes an embarrassment.

1   The anatomy of fraud

What is fraud?

The real definition of fraud is a question to which men have applied their minds for centuries.

Swift, in *Gulliver's Travels*, wrote: 'Care and vigilance, with a very common understanding, may preserve a man's goods from thieves, but honesty hath no fence against superior cunning.' Dr Michael Levi, an eminent lecturer in criminology, in an article for the *Police Review* (4 December, 1981) likened it to venereal disease. He wrote: 'Neither victims nor perpetrators want to talk about it; those who have encountered it are afraid to discuss it in case others think that they have been involved with it; and the absence of debate not only does not prevent it from spreading, but actually makes it more difficult to control.'

As recently as 50 years ago, fraud was not generally recognised by the police as a problem, but in London at about that time the first Fraud Squad, called The City of London and Metropolitan Police Company Fraud Department was set up to investigate what was seen then as a growing incidence of company fraud. Twenty years later the position had hardly changed but fraud squads similar to the one in London had been set up in some major provincial cities. The majority of police forces, however, still dealt with fraud as unsatisfactory business. More often than not they referred fraud victims to their civil remedy: they were advised to seek redress via the civil law and no criminal investigation was made.

It was not until the late 1960s that fraud became recognised by the police as a problem in all areas of the country. It was at that time that most police forces set up fraud squads to deal with a growing problem.

Even then, not all police forces recognised it as a real problem and the allocation of men and resources was minimal. The Office of the Director of Public Prosecutions at about that time dealt with fraud in the same way as with any other crime; they had no separate department to handle even large fraud cases, although specialist lawyers formed an unofficial nucleus of what was later to become the Fraud Division. They now have a large, efficient and very busy department dedicated exclusively to the investigation and prosecution of major fraud. Similarly the Department of Trade and Industry has a growing and efficient department charged with the investigation of business fraud.

A different crime

Fraud, to the victim, is often quite different from any other crime he may have experienced because the perpetrator may be someone well-known and trusted by him. Usually, the fraud victim finds it difficult to come to terms with the fact that it has happened; and that it was committed by a person he least expected to be involved. The perpetrator is often so well-known, liked and trusted that a decision to do anything about it is often very difficult to make; it is often felt that nothing should be done.

A recent fraud committed by a long serving, senior and trusted employee left the members of the company's board with what they saw as a very difficult decision. No one director wanted to make a decision on what should be done about the employee who was personally known to all of them. The facts were circulated to each director to determine what each thought was the best course of action. A summary of their thoughts, mainly in favour of dismissal but not prosecution, was sent to the chairman. He had no difficulty in coming to a decision. He wrote on the papers: 'We are not in the business of condoning fraud—prosecute.'

In this case the decision by the directors to recommend dismissal only had been influenced by the fact that the employee had himself reported the fraud to the managing director. He was the company accountant and had told the managing director that he had two pieces of news—one good, one bad. He said: 'I have prepared an analysis of the trading figures for the year and there is little doubt that we have made a greatly increased profit. The bad news is that because of personal financial difficulties I have been paying myself considerably more than my salary. It now amounts to such a large sum of money that I will be unable to pay it back. I have decided to tell you because if I don't the auditors will discover it and they will tell you.'

In another case a similarly long-serving and respected employee

2

had for many years been practising a fraud in the purchase department of a large manufacturing company. The fraud was discovered after he had left for a holiday cruise. His deputy decided in his absence to check some unusual papers he had found in the fraudster's desk. The auditors were called in to prepare an estimate of the fraud so that the financial director could confront the employee on his return from holiday. When the employee was seen by the financial director he admitted responsibility and wrote a cheque to repay the amount he was told he had stolen. The financial director decided to dismiss him on the spot, but as he had paid back what it was thought he had stolen no further action was to be taken: he would not be prosecuted. Whilst he had been away his fraudulent activities had been the talk of the factory. He had been employed for a very long time and was well known in all departments and by the people on the factory floor.

As soon as it became known that he would be dismissed but not prosecuted a shop steward asked to see the financial director. At the meeting the shop steward said that he was about to call a strike because he felt that factory workers were being discriminated against. He based this on the fact that a factory worker who had recently been caught stealing goods had been reported to the police for prosecution, whereas the white-collar worker who had defrauded the company was being allowed to get away with it. Telling the shop steward that the decision was based on the fact that the fraudster had paid back all the stolen money was a futile argument; the shop steward pointed out that they had also got back the goods stolen by the factory worker. The decision not to prosecute was reversed and the fraud was reported to the police. A full investigation revealed that the amount actually stolen was nearly treble the substantial amount the employee had repaid. The fraudster, confronted with this fact, readily admitted the additional amount and offered to repay it. He even offered to make out the cheque to the police officer investigating the fraud. He was prosecuted, pleaded guilty to the charges and when he appeared for sentence he blamed the company, alleging that they had treated him very badly for years.

He said he had been kept on a low salary and had been denied promotion, so to punish them he had devised the fraud to pay himself what he thought he was worth. He told the court that he had not spent any of the money and that he had repaid it all. He was given a suspended prison sentence and left the court a free man.

Although he had said that he was poorly paid and that he had paid back all the money stolen, on the day he left court he made a cash offer for a newsagent's shop directly opposite the factory gates.

Making a decision

A decision as to what course of action should be taken when someone is caught committing fraud is a difficult one. Some thought must be given to the point that if the offender is dismissed and not prosecuted he is free to seek other employment where his tendencies are not known, and, having learned by being caught once, he will be more careful and cunning with his next fraud.

Not everyone who commits an act which might be construed as fraud believes that what they are doing is wrong. Producing a balance sheet which conceals assets or liabilities in order that the company can continue trading, or pay a lower dividend, or less tax, is a defrauding of creditors, the Inland Revenue, or shareholders, and is a serious offence. The person committing such offences often believes he is doing it for everyone's good, and does not even consider that he might be committing fraud. If the annual profit of a company were simply the difference between the cost of what is bought and the income from what is sold, there would be few problems. But for this to be true a company would need to be started on January 1 and wound up on December 31. The annual loss or profit of a company is the difference between the net worth of the company shown in the balance sheet on day one and the net worth a year later. It is in valuing balance sheet items that the big difference of interpretation occurs. The sums involved in assets are so large in comparison with trading profits that small variations can make a huge impact on the profit declared. It has been shown that by treating the same company's accounts in two different ways there was a loss of £232,000 in one set of accounts which turned into a pre-tax profit of £1,634,000 in the second set.

Who commits fraud?

There is no indication that family background or personality type has a bearing on who commits fraud. Situation factors and social background are said to be crucial, as is knowledge and opportunity. Frauds have been committed by politicians (including former cabinet ministers), by titled persons, by ministers of religion of all denominations, by policemen, by lawyers, by employees and by businessmen.

A closer examination would probably reveal a much longer list of people and include almost every category of person who has the knowledge and the opportunity to commit fraud once he has decided to do so. Quite often the person who commits fraud has led a previously blameless and crime-free life. The fraud may start off as what he sees as only a 'borrowing' with every intention to pay back. Once, however, a fraudster has discovered how easy it is the borrowing gets bigger and the intention to repay weakens.

Most companies seek to recruit decent, honest and loyal people and try to help them stay that way by protecting them against fraud and frequent temptations. Temptations cannot be wholly eliminated and none of us is divine. Human frailty being what it is, there is a small proportion of people who occasionally have a brainstorm and go off the rails. They will not only steal the money; they will steal the headlines, if caught. With very rare exceptions they are not the perpetrators of carefully planned swindles. Usually they blunder into what appears to be salvation from financial difficulties. Fraud appears to be as habit-forming as the spending of easy money. After a while, fraudsters will be carrying out operations regularly and steadily perfecting their methods. In the end they may be caught as a consequence of over-confidence or over-sophistication.

Fraud is not really their element; they seldom have the turn of mind or inclination to invent a fraud but having found, often by accident, one method which works they stick to it. From an investigator's point of view this is useful; having carefully studied one example in a series it is then comparatively easy to look for repetitions of the pattern. Investigators normally find they are dealing with basically decent people who have suddenly strayed when faced with temptation. They are rarely dealing with embezzling master-minds capable of working out and executing a variety of intricate schemes planned in cold blood.

Where bribery is involved it is usually quite paltry in relation to the sum involved in the fraud, as a corrupted person does not stop to think just how much he is giving away.

Accident and coincidence

Very few frauds were ever thought up as a theoretical exercise. What has normally happened in the past is that a combination of accident and coincidence produces some quite unforseeable situation. Someone notices it, realises its implications for fraud, and then proceeds to achieve the same result by inducing the same accident or coincidence.

In his book *Other People's Money* (Wadsworth 1972) Donald Creasy, an American criminologist, identifies the belief in the mind of most convicted white-collar fraudsters that they are still honest. They were able to rationalise their criminal behaviour with their perception of themselves as honest people. A strange quirk, but one present in so many cases that it could neither be accidental, nor the result of sample bias. The convicted fraudsters invariably considered that the funds they had obtained by fraud were due to them; that they had merely borrowed the money, or considered their own behaviour less reprehensible than the way their employers were behaving. They had a non-criminal, inner rationalisation for their dishonesty.

This, of course, does not apply to someone who previously made a living by other crimes, such as robbery or burglary, but who then found that white-collar crime was more socially acceptable and carried less risk. These people often bring with them to their fraudulent activities some of the more violent and undesirable elements of their previous criminal activities. Take, for example, the company formed by criminals whose major part of the business is fraudulent, and whose credit controller may well be a muscle man.

In endeavouring to collect money owed to his company he will use threats of violence. It has been known for such a person to call on a company which has run into financial difficulty but owes his company money. They are unable to pay and are about to liquidate quite legitimately. The credit controller will demand immediate payment of the outstanding debt and will often back his demand with veiled or direct threats of violence or even death. One ploy he may use to re-inforce the threats is to leave a kidney donor's card with a suggestion that if the money is not available when he returns then it might be advisable to have filled in the card. When he does return, the credit controller will repeat the threats then suggest a way out of the problem. The threatened director may, by this time, be so intimidated that he is willing to listen to any suggestion, even fraudulent.

The suggestion is usually that the insolvent company should examine its list of debtors and if there is one owing a sum approaching the amount due to the credit controller's company then it should be assigned to his company. The assignment will be backdated since the company is about to go into liquidation. A copy letter will be prepared informing the debtor company that the debt has been assigned. The letter will not be sent to the unsuspecting company but will be inserted into the company files to back up the assignment in the event of query. In this way the criminal company is able to collect the money owed to it direct from the unsuspecting debtor company—money which would ordinarily be available for the benefit of the creditors. When the records of such criminally motivated companies are examined it is often found that there are many such assigned debts, and that they are often in respect of created debts owed to them by the insolvent company.

Long Firm Fraud

This does not necessarily mean that there is a Mafia-type problem in fraud in Britain. There is, however, little doubt that some very large frauds are organised and committed by groups of people who seek, and often find, very large rewards in the crime. A very popular area for this activity is in Long Firm Fraud, and links between groups of known and previously convicted persons can easily be established. It is also quite common for similar frauds in several parts of the country to be linked. This is particularly so in the area of the disposal of fraudulently obtained goods.

Long Firm Fraud is where fraudsters obtain goods on credit by falsely pretending to be in a large way of business. They have no intention of making more payments than are absolutely necessary to keep their business alive long enough for them to accumulate large quantities of goods for which they have no intention of paying. Generally, the goods are ordered from companies at a considerable distance from the fraudsters' operating base so that there are unlikely to be any visits from suppliers before any goods are despatched.

It is universally accepted that the majority of wholesale businesses can only be carried on with a credit system. The pressure of modern competition forces manufacturers to compete with others by offering lower prices and by granting larger and longer credit facilities. Fear of losing a prospective customer tends to lead traders into giving credit to customers without making full enquiries on their stability. These conditions play into the hands of the Long Firm Fraudsters.

In its simplest form the fraud is carried out by someone who starts a business and obtains his first supplies on the basis of cash payments or very short credit terms. For a time he pays bills regularly. He then takes advantage of the confidence created amongst his suppliers, sends much larger orders, obtains extended credit, and gradually lengthens the time before paying. When he reaches a point where he believes that he has obtained the maximum credit which will be allowed by his suppliers he disposes of the goods as rapidly as possible for cash and disappears with the proceeds.

There is a more complicated method, which has produced very high returns for the fraudsters, and which involves a number of persons who enter into a conspiracy to defraud their creditors. When the fraud is first started three or four companies are launched, usually off-the-shelf companies. Elaborately headed stationery is prepared, orders are placed and credit requested. Very often, but not always, the traders receiving the orders ask for references which ought to be followed up. But even some of those who ask for references fail to have them checked. If, however, a supplier does decide to follow up the references this will present no problem to the fraudsters. They will simply refer the request to one of their other companies, formed specifically for that purpose. In due course favourable references and first class accounts of creditworthiness and stability of the company are given.

The victims, of course, are unaware that their customers and the companies supplying the references are associated. There may also be a central warehouse, where all the fraudulently obtained goods are sent for disposal. This warehouse is usually disguised under another and possibly legitimate company name, and is the place from which the retailers purchase their goods. The warehouse company will have no obvious connections, other than trading, with the fraudulent companies, and false paid invoices showing full value having been paid for the goods will often have been prepared. The more sophisticated of these conspiracies may also have their own retail outlets purchasing their supplies from the company warehouse, but with no obvious connections, other than as customers, with the company or the warehouse.

The ultimate objective

Whether the fraud is carried out by the simple method or where there is a conspiracy the ultimate objective is the same—to defraud the suppliers. The goods are either sold for any price which can be obtained for them in cash, or they are moved to the central warehouse where the false paid invoices are prepared, and the swindlers make off with the proceeds, leaving the victims always poorer and sometimes wiser. The fraudsters may not always abscond however, particularly in a conspiracy, because they will probably have arranged for a front man who is prepared to face prison for a fee, to take the blame. The main conspirators will often hide the proceeds and trust to having a sympathetic liquidator. They will also hope to pass through any bankruptcy proceedings by using falsified books showing fictitious losses.

In order to carry out a Long Firm Fraud a fraudster will need capital, because he has to pay for initial purchases whilst he is establishing confidence with his suppliers. He has to pay the wages of staff such as warehousemen and drivers, and he may also have to pay rent for his premises, although the landlord usually ends up as a creditor at the conclusion of the fraud. The staff keeping the false books are usually family or co-conspirators. To start the fraud the fraudster may use an existing company which he has purchased for the purpose. This is the more usual thing to do although he might trade under a business name. In either case the longer the period for which the operator is able to obtain credit, and the more people he can trade with, the bigger the payoff. It is usual for the fraud to operate for between three to six months before the operation is closed down and the fraudsters move to new and better frauds.

Because they pose under the guise of legitimate business, and may have apparently excellent references, these frauds are difficult to spot in the early stages. Quite often, particularly where there is a conspiracy, they are prepared to trade legitimately for as long as is necessary. The fraudsters are usually expert at spotting suspicion; when they do they will extend their operation on a legitimate basis, or even abandon the fraud. If they are able to allay the suspicion and carry on trading the crash will come sooner or later.

The accompanying chart demonstrates the basic method of operating a Long Firm Fraud.

Anatomy of Long Firm Fraud

1   Backed by his own resources, or those of a syndicate Mr X provides capital to establish new business or acquires established concern with good credit rating to operate as a Long Firm Fraud.

2   A front man who will share in the proceeds of the fraud is installed as manager, director or proprietor of business. He will usually adopt a false identity. Mr X or someone representing his interests often present in the guise of warehouseman etc., to watch activities of front man.

3   Mr X makes available existing contacts with other fraudulent businessmen; or establishes and acquires other businesses for the purpose of providing false references as to the creditworthiness of business run by front man.

4   The front man:
(a) obtains goods on credit from suppliers;
(b) refers requests for trade references to concerns nominated by Mr X, and/or;
(c) makes prompt payment for initial small orders, enlarging scope of orders as suppliers' confidence increases.

5   He then disposes of goods in bulk and below cost to:
(a) dubious wholesalers and job lot buyers supplying cut price stores, market traders etc.;
(b) other concerns in which Mr X has a controlling interest; but provides invoices for realistic amounts to satisfy any enquiries until goods are disposed of when invoices will probably be destroyed. May deduct an agreed commission but greater part of proceeds is paid to Mr X.

6   The front man may:
(a) make a false report to police alleging theft of goods from the premises or in transit; or
(b) arrange for a serious fire at premises, then report stock destroyed. May claim from insurance company for stock allegedly stolen or destroyed, but to allay suspicions and enquiry often does not do so.

7   If aggrieved suppliers try to obtain judgment in civil courts, front man or solicitors instructed by him will often lodge spurious defences and thus prolong the life of the fraudulent business until the largest possible amount of credit has been obtained from remaining suppliers. When demands for payment become too pressing and no more credit can be obtained the front man severs connections and reassumes true identity. Business fails. If traced, front man may attribute failure of business to theft of goods or destruction of stock.

Liquidation fraud

It is often difficult to determine whether a company which has gone into liquidation owing money is a genuine failure or a fraud. This is because liquidation fraud is another very profitable area for the fraudster. The fraud may be committed either by the officers of the company, or by the liquidator, or by both acting together.

Where the fraud is committed by the officers of the company it can be that it is a legitimate company which has become insolvent for a variety of reasons. At that stage, a liquidation would not, of course, necessarily include fraud. Instead of seeking an honourable liquidation for the benefit of the creditors, in a liquidation fraud the company is often kept going for as long as possible whilst the directors clear their personal obligations. This often results in the deficiency being greater than it would have been had the company liquidated at the proper time. The directors will ensure that they are themselves solvent and able to set up again in business, probably in the same line. This is fraudulent trading and an offence under the Companies Acts. Quite often a new and similar company is set up before liquidation to trade with the insolvent company and has the same directors. The assets of the troubled company are gradually passed to the new company before it liquidates with little or nothing left for the creditors.

Fraudulent trading of this kind may sometimes be operated in collusion with the liquidator who will sell off any remaining assets from the troubled company to the new company at a knock-down price. In many cases, a company is set up with the specific intention of stripping assets before going into liquidation, only to trade again under the guise of a new company, and may even strip the assets a second or third time from succeeding companies.

Liquidation fraud was becoming so prevalent that the Insolvency Act of 1985 was introduced with the express purpose of controlling the activities of liquidation fraudsters who, more often than not, were never prosecuted for any offences. The Act enables persons who were the directors of liquidated companies, in certain circumstances, to be disqualified from holding the office of director.

It has also become increasingly necessary to control the activities of liquidators. During the 1980s it was becoming common for persons to set up as liquidators with the sole intention of realising as much of the assets of insolvent companies as possible. The realisation of these assets was not to be for the benefit of the creditors of the liquidated company but for themselves. Many fraudulent liquidators made themselves a great deal of money before controls on their activities were introduced; many of them are now living lives of luxury abroad.

Outside fraud

There are two areas of fraud from outsiders which can affect almost any business but which may not be very easily detected. The first is quite small insofar as the fraud on each individual business is concerned, but when each small fraud is added together it becomes very substantial. The fraudulent directory became a lucrative business for fraudsters when they discovered that by sending invoices for entries in a directory instead of asking people if they wished to be included they were often paid without question. From this small beginning many small organisations set up in the business of producing Business Directories then sending out invoices to unsuspecting companies demanding payment for an entry which was made to appear as a genuine reprint of a previous entry. These invoices were unsolicited and the victims often paid without realising that they were not subscribers to the publication.

The practice became so widespread that legislation was introduced to make such unsolicited invoices unlawful unless they contained a section, easily readable, which told the recipient that the document was not an invoice but a request for an order. There were some successful prosecutions but the majority of the fraudsters simply moved their activities overseas and continued to send out unsolicited invoices in the same way. It has become so prevalent, because it is so lucrative a business, that the London Fraud Squad has a section specially charged with dealing with this type of fraud. The directory frauds have received wide publicity, but companies still pay without realising that they are the victims of an elaborate swindle.

The second area is a little different in that instead of an invoice an order is sent for such things as high value machinery to be shipped to a port in an African country. These orders emanate from the African country and are sent to companies around the world. They are usually accompanied by a banker's draft drawn on the international department of a well known major bank, the draft being payable when the goods are delivered to the African port. The address given for the bank, however, is fictitious and the whole draft, from wording to stamps and acceptances, is forged. As with the directory frauds, not every person who receives such an order is deceived, but some companies do despatch goods before they discover that the whole operation is fraudulent. As with the directory frauds, and similar publicity the fraud continues and unsuspecting victims are being caught out.

The fraudster, by the very nature of his crimes, is a plausible and very often a likeable person, because otherwise he would not get away with it. His intention is to gain the confidence of his victim, and it is often the case that even after being defrauded many victims refuse to believe it of the person responsible. In a recently investigated case where many people had between them invested several millions of pounds, very few would believe that they had been defrauded even though they had lost their total investments. One reason for this was that the fraudster was good at his trade and had gone to a lot of trouble to set up palatial offices, fitted with computers, always manned and working, which investors were sometimes invited to visit to discuss their investments. There were many staff working at the offices, and all investors had been advised of profits made on their investments. They were offered the profits in cash, or were invited to re-invest to make more profit.

It all looked very good, but the investors did not know that the so-called employees were all innocent agency staff who never remained working for the company long enough to get to know anything of consequence. They were employed to research world markets but never became involved in the actual investments. This was because there were no real investments; the whole set up was totally fraudulent and the so-called profits were also fictitious and paid out of the victims' own investments. One day the fraudster did not appear at his offices and over three million pounds of investors' money vanished.

At risk from fraud

An analysis of reported cases has shown that the most common perpetrator of frauds in companies is a manager, closely followed by accounts officials, with directors and/or partners not very far behind.

It seems that it automatically follows that if you are in business you are at risk from fraud, certainly from insiders who either deliberately or by chance seize an opportunity to steal your money. There is, however, another factor which increases the chances of being a victim of fraud: corruption. In many countries business relationships may often be preceded by gifts which are intended to incline the receiver to look more favourably upon the giver when it comes to doing business. Pre-business giving has not always been common in Britain, but over the last few years it has become far more common, and more acceptable.

Bribery or corruption occurs when a gift or consideration, is given and received with the intention that it will influence the receiver in favour of the giver. It takes place, usually, in the secret personal knowledge of both parties and only they know the true intention. It is the surrounding circumstances in which it is given and received which will show whether or not it is intended to corrupt. If, for instance, a substantial sum of money or an expensive holiday is given, it is more than probable that the gift is intended to corrupt. If, however, the gift is merely a single gin and tonic, not too many people would be corrupted by it, but they might if the gift were a case of gin or whiskey. It is not merely a matter of degree, but of the circumstances in which the gift is given and the intention behind the giving and the receiving. It is often the case that many businesses unknowingly pay far more for their goods than they should because a supplier has made corrupt gifts to employees of the purchasing company. A corrupt supplier increases a company's risk of fraud and turns corrupted employees of the purchasing company into traitors. They are no longer working for their employers but against them; whilst the employee may enjoy, it is hoped temporarily, a more expensive life style, the corrupting supplier is enjoying profits which should rightfully belong to the victim company.

The payment of reasonable expenses for services rendered differs only in degree from a payment which might be thought to amount to bribery and corruption. Similarly, payment of a generous salary or expenses to company executives may differ only in form from the unlawful abstraction of corporate funds by those involved. To this end it is often not the substance of what is done, but the manner in which it is done, that matters. No one is entirely immune from fraud; it crops up in small and large companies, it involves small and large amounts, it is perpetrated by management, by both senior and junior employees, and to be a victim of fraud is often a devastating experience.

The cost of fraud

In a survey entitled *The Incidence, Reporting and Prevention of Commercial Fraud,* sponsored jointly by the The Police Foundation, Arthur Young and the Home Office (March 1986), Dr Michael Levi found that commercial fraud recorded by the London Fraud Squads represents almost three times the total cost of all other property crimes in London. He found that almost 40 per cent of the companies involved in the survey had reported at least one fraud costing over £50,000.

When a fraud is discovered and the fraudster is confronted with the fact he rarely accepts that the amount the victim says is the total loss from the fraud is the amount he has stolen. He believes that it is substantially less because it is unusual for a fraudster himself to calculate the total yield from his fraud as he is concerned only with the amount he can get away with at any one time. He himself is often appalled when he discovers, or is told, the real extent of his fraud. Nevertheless, fraudsters have caused companies to go into liquidation, caused individuals to become bankrupt, and have even caused countries to have serious financial problems.

Many of the people who have been charged with offences amounting to fraud have, when arrested, owned at least one Rolls Royce, or have been living in circumstances far above the capacity of their legitimate income. Fortunes have been made by stealing small amounts of money over a long period of time, or from many sources. One of the most well known computer frauds in the United States involved stealing the odd cent from interest paid on many bank accounts; the gain for the fraudster was many millions of dollars. Neither the Department of Trade and Industry, the Director of Public Prosecutions, nor the police routinely compile statistics on the cost of fraud. It would, in any case, be extremely difficult and not very accurate because the amounts taken by fraudsters do not always represent the total losses by fraud over any given period of time. There is what has been called 'the hidden face of fraud' — frauds which have never been discovered, and those which have never been reported. The amounts involved could well be as much, if not more, than the figures for reported fraud.

An attempt was made in 1980 to compile statistics for fraud and the results were staggering compared with losses due to other property thefts. In the year 1980 recorded losses due to theft, burglary and robbery in the whole of England and Wales totalled £550 million. Of this, in London alone, £50 million was lost through burglary and £2 million by robbery, whereas the London Fraud Squads dealt with £400 million in fraud. A further £100 million can be added for the provincial areas. Additionally there was: £400 million of income tax evasion; £1,070 million of VAT fraud: £170 million of social security fraud and £70 million from untaxed vehicles. The cost of fraud can be measured only in cash; it would be impossible to measure the extent of the misery caused by the activities of fraudsters.

The law on fraud

There is no real definition of fraud in criminal law. Neither is there a specific offence of fraud with which a criminal can be charged. The essentials of offences like murder, theft or burglary have been established and accepted for centuries. The same cannot be said of fraud because the boundaries of what is acceptable and unacceptable conduct are constantly changing.

The two leading branches of law in Britain are civil law and criminal law, both of which may be involved in fraud cases. Civil law relates to disputes between individuals, affecting only themselves, whilst criminal law is concerned with acts and omissions affecting the community at large. In most fraud cases there is an element of civil law which can be pursued, but this often takes second place to the criminal law issues. In virtually all cases criminal law requires a particular intent or state of mind as a necessary ingredient of a criminal offence. The prosecution of transgressors against the criminal code is primarily the responsibility of the police, whilst in civil law action is the responsibility of the disputing parties.

Civil law disputes are usually adjudicated by members of the judiciary sitting alone and deciding themselves on the liability or otherwise of the parties appearing before them. An offending party, prosecuted under criminal law is judged by his peers acting as a jury, with the judiciary controlling the admissibility or otherwise of facts alleged against the conduct of offenders. This does not mean that the boundaries are clearly defined as in certain areas both the civil and criminal law merge. This has enabled police officers with no facilities for investigating fraud to write off reported cases as civil dispute and to refer complaints to a civil law remedy.

Although there is no actual definition, or specific offence, of fraud in criminal law the Theft Act 1968 (sections 15–20) is an important piece of relevant legislation. A common characteristic of offences contained in the Act is the purpose of the offender to obtain a material advantage, or financial advantage, by some deceptive practice.

Section 15 deals with a person who, by any deception, dishonestly obtains property belonging to another, with the intention of permanently depriving the other of it. Hence the often stated intention of the fraudster that it was only a borrowing or 'I only intended to teach them a lesson'. This section covers all kinds of property including money, and where a conviction is obtained for an offence against the section the offender is liable to be sent to prison for up to ten years. 'Obtaining' is clearly defined in the Act, and a person is to be treated as obtaining property if he takes ownership, possession or control of it, and includes circumstances in which it is obtained for another, or enables another, to obtain or retain the property.

An example of this was a recent case where someone in the United States wanted to send a small sum of money to a young relative in Britain. He arranged this through an American bank. When the transfer details were worked out the clerk in the American bank inadvertently put the decimal point in the wrong place, adding too many noughts to the figure. The result was that instead of £297 being transferred to the recipient's account the actual credit to the account was £297,000.

Until this large credit arrived, the young relative's account had been very modest and the manager of the bank was surprised when the money arrived. He informed the recipient who in turn told an uncle about it. The uncle made very quick arrangements with the boy for the money to be withdrawn from the account, secretly disposed of all of it, then disappeared for several days. The mistake made by the American bank was discovered but when the disappearing uncle was arrested all the money had gone. He claimed that he thought the money was intended for him as the proceeds of the sale of his house. He could not explain why it was credited via the United States, why it was credited to his nephew's account, or how it coincided with the mistake made by the American bank. He was convicted of obtaining the money by deception, not from the American bank but from the British bank, and was sent to prison. The money was never recovered, and as no court order was made for compensation or restitution the American bank must have had recourse to civil law.

'Deception' is also clearly defined in the Theft Act, and deception means whether it is deliberate or reckless, and can be made by words or conduct as to fact or law. This includes a deception as to the present intentions of the person using the deception or any other person. This means that where an employee deliberately passes for payment an invoice which he knows to be false in that it is for goods which have never actually been supplied, or for a greater amount than is actually due to the benefit of the supplier, then he has practised a deception on his employer.

Until fairly recently a false pretence, which is the same as a deception, had to be in relation to a past or present fact, but this now extends to an intention such as a promise to the future, and may be deliberate as well as reckless. It is often difficult in fraud cases to pin down responsibility on particular individuals, as in criminal law the guilt or innocence of the defendant is related to his precise mental state, and it is often difficult to establish precise states of mind such as intention, recklessness and negligence in relation to individual offenders. Where the case involves a series of complex transactions by a number of individuals at various levels in a company it is considerably more difficult.

The Theft Act also covers fraudulent offences such as obtaining a pecuniary advantage by deception (an example would be obtaining a loan or overdraft by giving false information as to status or future prospects); false accounting (making an entry in an account which would falsely indicate that an amount had been received or paid) and deals with the liability of company officers, in relation to their duties within the company. But the main Acts which regulate the way a business is conducted and the duties of company directors are the Companies Acts. In the prosecution of fraud, criminal penalties in the Companies Acts and related legislation have been relied on for many years, and there is a range of different offences covering almost every aspect of company administration.

There appears to be no consistency in the formulation of criminal offences to deal with particular fraudulent abuses, leaving law enforcement agencies with a ragbag of weapons, some of which have been likened to a blunderbuss and others to a toothpick, to deal with some of the most complex offences and sophisticated offenders that are likely to be encountered in the whole field of criminal law. Prosecuting authorities often fall back on such general common law charges as conspiracy to defraud, either as a primary count or as an additional 'roll up' count. Where substantive charges can be made judges do not generally like conspiracy counts, but the advantage of such charges is that the evidence which can be given is often more general than in a specific count of theft or deception, and this tends to give a more complete overall picture of what actually happened. Very often, however, where no charge other than conspiracy can be brought there may well be no prosecution.

In fraud, it is a fact that even when the intricacies of the various transactions have been unravelled, and admissible evidence to establish the parts played by the various defendants has been collected, the task of enforcement is by no means complete. There are further problems in the selection of an appropriate charge or charges which will give the court a true picture of what really happened, and in bringing a prosecution to a successful conclusion. It is often difficult to establish the elements of an offence which matches the seriousness of the alleged fraud and thus to secure an appropriate penalty, but this does not absolve the prosecution from the obligation to lay before the court the full details of what are often exceedingly complex operations.

The investigation of fraud, however, has slowly caught up with the 20th century, and investigations by all agencies are far more sophisticated now than they were some years ago. This is also happening in the law, and with fraud becoming an established practice, even sometimes in the board room, the law will alter to meet modern day needs.

2   Minor fraud

Major or minor?

The Roman philosopher Seculus said: 'Only weak eyes weep at another's misfortune'. This can apply to the fraudster who only rarely sees the misfortunes he has inflicted on his victim. He certainly does not weep, except at his own misfortune when caught. Many weep or express concern about their own misfortunes, and the effects on their own wife and family, but concern for the victim is rarely present, and never expressed. In court, a fraudster will often blame his victim for tempting him into fraud, or for putting him into a situation where he felt he had little option but to commit fraud. This applies in both small and large frauds, and to most categories of fraudster, except possibly the professional.

Fraud is often referred to as either 'minor' or 'major' but it is difficult to find a dividing line between these two categories. For instance, can minor fraud be divided from major fraud by the amount of money involved? Can they be divided by the scale of the fraud? Or can they be divided by the number of people defrauded, or by the number of fraudsters involved? Fraud is a devastating thing to happen to anyone, but one person's loss may be, to him, a minor fraud; to the next person a similar loss may be a major fraud, as well as a total catastrophe. It is not so very long ago that talk of a million pound fraud would call for a major investigation. Now, with modern business talking in multi-millions of pounds, a fraud involving a million pounds may not even be classed by either victim or investigator as a major fraud merely because of the amount involved. Many frauds are complicated by the way in which they have been committed; they require painstaking and expert investigation, even when the amount involved is comparatively small, but they need not necessarily be classed as major fraud. Any fraud can, like a business, be expanded and developed if the opportunities and the availibility of money is right. What may start out as a minor fraud, and if discovered in its early stages may remain a minor fraud,

21

may after a period of time become a major fraud. It will usually, however, when analysed, still be the same simple basic fraud.

It is quite possible that most people in business at some time in their careers have had first hand experience of minor fraud—as a spectator or victim rather than as a perpetrator. Examples likely to have been encountered would include an employee on night shift using the company's telephone to ring his family in New Zealand. There is no need for him to conceal the call because the telephone account is not closely controlled. Other examples include the misuse and theft of office supplies and equipment, or the misuse of computer time. Such frauds are usually very minor in any well ordered company and are perpetrated only by an employee with no direct responsibility or accountability for the company assets. Such frauds usually result in a daily erosion of profit, rather than a high impact or spectacular loss. Even so they should not be overlooked since this type of fraud is committed by people who can readily graduate to larger things.

Teeming and lading

Another form of crime involves manipulation of accounting records. This is usually carried out by employees who do have access to, and control of, accounting records, but whose regular access to physical assets is limited. A typical example of this fraud is teeming and lading. It takes place when a cashier removes a sum of money from the daily bankings, leaves it off the record, then makes up the shortage from the cash received the following day. Another method which can be used is when cash shortage is concealed by fictitious posting to customers' accounts. Cash stolen need not necessarily be made up from subsequent receipts if the thief has access to both cash and sales ledgers. Teeming and lading often starts with the borrowing of a small amount and the intention to replace it on pay day. However, by the time the thief gets round to thinking about repaying, the amount stolen has probably become too high and the fraud continues until it is discovered.

Other frauds which fall into this category are the use of company machines, equipment or time to perform private or conflicting work, or the theft of tools, raw materials and working stocks. Shoplifting has always been looked on as a particularly high loss area in retail theft, but a recent analysis has shown that whilst the average loss from shoplifting is £40 for each theft, dishonest workers take an average £1,000 worth of goods. The extent of the problem can be seen from the figures for recovered stolen property. Property worth £10 million is recovered nationally from shoplifters, and a further £18 million worth from employees. Not all dishonest employees work in the retail trade: office goods and materials are equally attractive to thieves.

Collusion

Fraud can be committed by suppliers, customers or contractors in collusion with employees through a business relationship. A typical example is where a supplier submits false invoices and has an accomplice working in collusion with him to authorise the invoices for payment. Manipulation is usually confined to those documents and accounts which pass between the fraudulent company and the colluding employee as a result of their business relationship.

It is recognised that corporate fraud results from a combination of motivational and situational factors in which the critical point is the presence of an opportunity. A criminally-inclined employee is likely to exploit an opportunity when he perceives a low chance of detection. But fraud is committed for many different reasons, the main difference being the type of person who commits it. It may be that a fraud is committed by an otherwise honest businessman who does so in the belief that he is saving his business from collapse and himself from bankruptcy. It may be committed by an employee who has been with the company for many years and who sees an opportunity to enrich himself at the company's expense. It may be committed by that same employee because he is incompetent and needs to commit fraud in order to keep his job. It may even be committed by someone in a position of trust who has been corrupted by an outside source, such as a supplier. There are also those who commit fraud as a way of earning their living, or simply because they enjoy the risks as well as the rewards of fraud. But to whichever category a fraudster belongs he will rarely agree that his reason for committing fraud was greed.

Very few frauds are original in concept, but there are always people who think up new variations on an old theme, and different ways of committing old established kinds of fraud. Whilst it may be possible from the particular type of business to determine the kind of fraud to which it might fall victim, it is impossible to forecast whether or not it will happen, or for what reason. In most businesses the odds are that at some time someone will attempt to commit fraud. Whilst it is difficult to be absolutely sure, even with precautions, that you will never be defrauded, a knowledge of what others have suffered and the means used to commit fraud, can be a guide and a help.

Examples

The examples given are of frauds which have been committed and will serve as a guide to what might be happening if fraud is suspected in a company. Some of the frauds described were committed by employees, some by businessmen, and others by professional fraudsters, but all are of the type which might well be classified as minor fraud. One fraud was committed by an employee who was overpromoted and incompetent, another by an employee who felt he had been badly treated by his employers.

The businessmen fraudsters include an example of a fraud committed to save a collapsing and insolvent business. Another fraud was committed by the businessman who saw an opportunity to make a lot of money and expand his business by using fraudulent means. So far as the professional swindlers are concerned, one group saw the public as their victim, and another saw legitimate business as their victim. Whilst the effect of fraud on a person who is a victim does not necessarily mean the collapse of his business, it can often destroy the trust in people which he may have spent a lifetime building, and the first case is concerned with such a man.

Employee fraud

The victim in this case had spent many years running a successful and profitable company, which he sold when he felt it was time for him to retire. Rather than retire completely he bought a very successful and popular restaurant and club near his retirement home. This was a smaller business than his previous one so that he was able to be involved but in a much less demanding capacity than before.

When the new owner took over there was a full complement of staff in the restaurant, and most of them stayed on to work for him. The new owner was happy with his retirement venture and he was successful at it; a very happy working relationship grew between him and his staff. After a time he needed to recruit additional staff and he recruited from amongst those who had worked for him in his previous business. In most cases these people proved to be loyal, hardworking and trusted servants, but one was to become a fraudster and by his activities destroy his victim's retirement happiness.

Amongst those recruited from the previous business was a stock keeper. For two years he was able to give an appearance of being competent at his work. He fitted well into the pattern of things, going quietly about his business, and was responsible to the old restaurant manager who had remained when the new owner took over. After about two years the manager wanted to improve his position, and as there was little opportunity for this where he now worked he gave due notice of his intention to leave.

The owner had to look for a replacement manager, and, as he was happy with his existing staff, he looked among them for a successor. For a time he ran the restaurant himself, and was assisted in this by the man he had employed as a resident stock keeper. This man proved to be a very willing assistant; he was always available when needed, and as a result of this he was rewarded by having his salary increased. Eventually, he was appointed to the vacant post of manager. A new, part-time, non-resident stock keeper was taken on to do the work previously performed by the new manager, and he was required to report his stocktake figures directly to the manager.

The new manager was given full control of the restaurant including the purchase of supplies: the owner reverted to his former low profile capacity. The choice of suppliers was left to the manager, and he was expected to purchase only sufficient to ensure the success of the restaurant. He was also required to examine all invoices from the suppliers and to prepare their bills for payment by the owner at the end of each month. He received all the invoices from the suppliers and recorded them in a duplicate book, with a separate page for each supplier. He was thus aware at the end of each month how much was owed to each supplier and he drew cheques for the amounts owed; these were then presented to the owner for signature.

For 18 months or so the owner was happy, trusting in the belief that his restaurant was successful, his profit margins adequate, and his staff competent. He was particularly pleased with his choice for the new manager who seemed to be running the place very well while keeping his suppliers' bills quite low. He did not think to ask how this was being done, even though he knew that there was great customer satisfaction in the value of the meals supplied. He assumed he had the right people in the right jobs. He was so pleased with the job being done by his manager and with the profits being made that he altered the manager's salary structure to give him a percentage of the very high profits which were apparently being made since he had taken over. There was a provision on the manager's profit share that he must ensure that good stocks were maintained. The non-resident stocktaker was required to visit the restaurant at the end of each month to take stock. Having done so, he provided the owner with a copy of his stocktake sheets. He also prepared a trading account showing the gross profit for each department, including the restaurant, and a profit and loss account showing the net profit for the period. For this purpose he had access to the sales day book from which to extract details of takings; details of purchases for the restaurant were given to him by the manager and they showed what purported to be total purchases in quantity and cost for each month. It was on these figures that the owner determined whether or not good stocks were being maintained, how well the restaurant was doing, and what percentage of profit was to be paid to the manager.

The auditors arrive

For a long time everything appeared to be in order. The first intimation that all was *not* well came when the auditors visited after the new manager had been in his post for about 18 months. They were given two sets of purchase analysis sheets which they were unable to reconcile. One set was given to them by the manager and was in fact an accurate and true record of the actual purchases made and their cost. The other set of analysis sheets was given to them by the owner and had been prepared by the part-time stocktaker, but it was totally different to those supplied by the manager as the figures for purchases were considerably less.

The sheets supplied by the owner showed that a very considerable profit had been made, but the sheets supplied by the manager, if true, meant that no profit at all had been made and the restaurant had actually made a substantial loss.

The owner was unable to explain the differences in the two sets of sheets, and at first the part-time stocktaker was under suspicion. The auditors, together with the owner, decided to confront both the stocktaker and the manager at a joint interview to see if any explanation would be forthcoming. Arrangements were made for a meeting the following day. Everyone turned up—except the manager who had disappeared. Everyone thought he had made off with ill-gotten gains because, by this time, an examination of the cheque book stubs had revealed quite large differences between the figures he provided and the actual cheques paid to the suppliers.

The manager was eventually traced to a seaside resort where he had for a time stayed in a run-down guest house. At the time of his arrest he was found to be destitute and had been admitted to a mental hospital apparently suffering from mental exhaustion. This fact was used quite blatantly at his subsequent trial.

How he did it

Following the manager's arrest, it was first necessary to establish what he had actually done, and how he did it. It was all quite simple. Like all good fraudsters before him he had relied upon the trust placed in him by his employer. He had completely deceived the owner into believing that he was employing a competent and honest manager, with the result that everything he did was believed and very little was checked. What he had actually done was to purchase far more supplies than were recorded on the analysis sheets given to the stocktaker. When he gave the owner the duplicate books recording the purchases made from each supplier, and the drawn cheques for signature, he supported each one with only a small selection of the actual invoices received, therefore showing a smaller total amount of supplies purchased. The totals on the duplicate book sheets agreed with the drawn cheques; the owner had no way of knowing that there were other invoices which had not been recorded but which needed to be paid. They also agreed with the figures produced by the stocktaker, so no suspicions were aroused.

What he actually did was to make out his duplicate book entry for most of the goods supplied, but left off several invoices, in one case totalling an additional £1,000 for that month. The entry total in the duplicate book showed that £996.30 was owed to the supplier instead of £1996.30. The cheque was drawn for the lower amount and when it had been signed by the owner it was returned to the manager for despatch. After the cheque had been signed, but before it was sent to the supplier, it was a simple matter for the manager who had written the cheque to alter the figures from 996 to 1996, and the words 'nine hundred pounds' to 'nineteen hundred pounds', which was the amount actually due. The analysis sheets given to the stocktaker for the owner showed the lower figures for each supplier, but the ones the manager kept himself showed the true position. He repeated this with most of the suppliers, so that the total purchases each month were considerably understated, and the profit margins inflated. The suppliers were paid their money, the owner thought he was running a successful and profitable business, and the manager kept his job and got his share of the inflated profit.

After the fraud had been running for some time he sometimes did not bother to forge the cheque. He simply presented the true figures to the owner in the duplicate book, supported by all the invoices, and together with a properly drawn cheque. In this case he would, after the cheque had been signed, make out new duplicate book entries leaving off several invoices which caused the stocktaker quite innocently to produce for the owner totally false profit figures.

Why he did it

Once it had been established *how* he had done it, it was necessary to establish *why*. It very soon became evident from the investigation that he had not, as was at first thought, made a large sum of money for himself. In fact except for his salary increases and his shares of the false profits, he had not made a penny for himself out of the payments to the suppliers. After he had disappeared his office was searched and a fairly substantial sum of money was found in an envelope in his office safe. At first there appeared to be no other explanation than that it was part of the proceeds of his fraud which he was unable to take with him when he left. However, when confronted with the money his explanation was in keeping with his other rather unusual activities. He explained that he had been instructed by the owner to obtain some of his purchases from a supplier whom the owner thought to be competitive with the others, but was in fact a supplier the manager had ceased to trade with about twelve months previously. In keeping with his other conduct he did not argue with the owner, but he did not follow his instructions and buy supplies from the suggested supplier. What he did do was to look up some old invoices from that supplier and alter the dates to make it appear that they were recent purchases. He made out a duplicate book entry as if they were current invoices and prepared a drawn cheque for the total amount shown, and this was signed by the owner.

After the cheque had been signed by the owner it was a simple matter for the manager to destroy both the duplicate book entry and the signed cheque. As no entry was made on the stocktaker's copy of the analysis sheets it was not included in the figures used to work out the profits and everyone was happy. This was the theory, but on one occasion things did not go as planned and the false cheque was inadvertently despatched to the supplier and the cheque banked. The suppliers themselves soon discovered that the money was not owed to them and telephoned the manager who asked them to return the cheque. This they agreed to do, but as it had already been banked they were unable to do so. Instead they sent their own cheque for the same amount of money.

This left the manager with a dilemma but his cunning was equal to it. When he received the supplier's cheque he asked the cashier to exchange it for cash from the previous night's restaurant takings and the cheque was paid into the restaurant's bank without raising any questions. He did not have to return the cheque to the supplier who would have become suspicious, but it did leave him with the problem of what to do with the money which he now had. He deliberated over this for some time but could not come up with a satisfactory answer. In the end he put the money in an envelope and left it in the safe where it remained until found by the owner after the fraud had been discovered.

What, then, was the motive for this elaborate fraud, which had caused the owner considerable loss, but had yielded nothing for the fraudster? The only explanation the fraudster gave was that he did it 'to keep the peace'. This was a very strange explanation, but as he had not made anything for himself in spite of the large sums of money involved, the only conclusion that could be drawn was that he had done it in order to keep his job. He turned out to be totally incompetent as manager but a far better fiddler.

At his trial he pleaded guilty to all the charges, but entered a plea of mitigation. This took the form of a totally unjustified attack on the owner alleging that it was entirely his fault that the fraud had taken place. The owner was branded as a tyrant for expecting the manager to operate within the confines placed upon him, and as a man who expected the impossible from his employees. Had this sort of allegation been made in evidence, rather than in mitigation, it would have been a simple matter to refute, as many witnesses would have given evidence to the contrary. As it was, the fraudster was able virtually to get away with it. As he had made nothing for himself other than the share of the false profits, and as he had spent some time in custody following his arrest and whilst awaiting trial, he did not get a prison sentence.

Supervisor fraud

Introducing new accounting systems as an addition to, instead of a replacement of, the old without a full appraisal, can often lead to disaster. It often means that employees who were involved with the old system have an advantage over those who know only the new system. If one of those older employees has a grudge, or feels that he has been badly treated, he is in a position where he can commit fraud almost with impunity. The case which will now be examined involved such a change in system. The employee committed his fraud over a period of four years, almost from the time of the introduction of the new system.

The man who was to commit this fraud had worked for a very large manufacturing company for over 30 years and, at the time of his offences, he was a supervisor in the Bought Ledger Department, part of the Purchases Department. Because of his long experience with the company in the same department he was in a unique position, having started his employment in the days when all purchases were entered into the ledger by hand. During his employment he had seen, or been part of, the change-over in systems right up to the introduction of a computer. He was known to have such a comprehensive working knowledge of the systems that anything he did or said within his section, or for that matter the department, was rarely questioned. He could almost control or alter the system as he wished.

His knowledge of the whole system was so comprehensive that he was able to intercept and substitute documents at any stage, either properly or improperly. The main factor which assisted his fraud was that the company installed a computer to help with a very large purchases budget, but also retained the old machine accounting system. One of the main factors which prompted him to commit fraud was the fact that even when this very new system was introduced, and in spite of his knowledge and seniority, others were promoted but not him. He had the sole responsibility to resolve transactions which were rejected by the computer into an error cycle, pipeline or suspense account. This, whilst instrumental in the fraud, was not his main responsibility which was to ensure that suppliers of goods were paid against accounts rendered.

Monthly settlement

The company had a very large number of suppliers and it was their policy to ensure where possible that payments were made monthly to clear the accounts. Each supplier was allocated an account number based on the initial letter of the supplier's name followed by a number relating to his position on the list of suppliers. This account number would never be allocated to any other supplier, even if the company ceased trading with them. This was another significant factor in the fraud. Most suppliers were paid by credit transfer to their banks at the end of each month and, to facilitate this, the clearing house code for each supplier's bank branch was recorded on his account. This last item was to be a significant factor in the detection of the fraud.

The invoices were checked on receipt and, if found to be correct, they were passed for payment and fed into the computer ready for the end-of-month accounts to be prepared. At a particular date in the month the computer was activated to produce the monthly accounts: the machine accounting system was then brought into use to produce remittance advices and a total payment sheet which would be sent to the company's bank. At this stage the customer's name and address did not appear on the documents. This was added afterwards on an addressograph machine which also recorded the customer's bank code on the same document. Before they reached this stage, however, they were checked for accuracy by the fraudster who was required to correct any mistakes, and for this a manual system was used: new remittance advices would be prepared on a typewriter.

This served to ensure that the suppliers were paid the correct

31

amount, or that the correct supplier was paid, but it still left the error in the computer, and on the computer-produced Bought Ledger. To correct this the details of the amendments would be entered on an Amendments to Master Sheet, ready for the next computer run. When this information was fed into the computer it would serve to adjust the Bought Ledger, but this was to prove another significant factor in the fraud.

The fraudster very rarely took a holiday; when he did he usually stayed at home and found excuses to go to the office several times. No one thought this unusual because of the type of man he was. He did, however, go on one holiday cruise which meant that he was unable to visit the office on a day crucial to his fraud. This was when it came to light. His deputy, although an able man, had not been with the company as long as the fraudster, and during the supervisor's absence the deputy was allowed to assume only partial responsibility for the supervisor's work. He was not allowed to touch the amendments sheets. With the supervisor on his cruise the deputy needed some documents to check a query which could not wait. Having checked everywhere else to locate the missing documents the deputy looked in the supervisor's desk drawers. He did not find the documents he needed, but he *did* find two copies of remittance advices which appeared to him very unusual. They had bank codes referring to savings banks, the sort which would be unlikely to be used by companies supplying goods. He decided to check them out and found that the names of the suppliers were unknown to him, and did not agree with the suppliers' codes shown on them. He also noticed that the names of the alleged suppliers were similar to the name of the supervisor. He checked the folders for the accounts which should have been those referred to by the codes and found that they were suppliers who had been discontinued some years previously. He reported what he had found to a superior and the auditors were called in to do a further check. They were able to advise that a fraud had probably been committed by the supervisor and suggested that he should be interviewed on his return from holiday. The company's financial director decided to conduct the interview himself. The returning supervisor readily admitted what he had done and offered to repay the money he was accused of stealing. He said that the money had been paid on a regular monthly basis into two bank accounts in his own name. He had also used two different systems to effect the transfers, but was not at that stage prepared to explain how he had done it.

Management did not press too hard for either disclosure of the system used, or for prosecution. They would have been happy to accept repayment on the total the auditors had assessed as stolen. The financial director, at first, accepted this course of action and it was agreed that if the fraudster paid the company a sum of money equivalent to that the auditors had alleged was stolen he would be dismissed but not prosecuted.

However, there had been a lot of talk within the department about the fraud and this leaked out onto the factory floor. The result was that a union representative approached the financial director about the plight of a factory hand in similar circumstances. The hand had been caught stealing, been dismissed and the facts reported to the police for prosecution. There was a threat of a strike and the decision not to prosecute the fraudster was quickly reversed and a criminal enquiry commenced.

Crude and risky

It was first necessary to establish what the supervisor had actually done. It soon became obvious that in the early days of his fraud he had used a method which was a little crude and risky, but he got away with it for some time before he perfected a safer method. He discovered that after the computer had been introduced when he made mistakes in rectifying errors in respect of suppliers who had been wrongly paid, his own mistakes on the amendments sheet were undiscovered until he did his own check. By playing about with some of these amounts and posting them to various unused accounts he found that he could build up credits which were available for manipulation.

It was not long before he made his first attempt at passing them out via the credit transfer system into unused accounts which he had transferred to his own bank code, and found that he received a credit into his bank account. In his first attempts he actually transferred monies received by way of credit from a supplier, or collected from an internal source into an unused account. Once the money was in the supplier's account he had credit transfer documents prepared and these passed through the system quite easily without being detected. He still needed to ensure that the money was transferred to his bank account and not to that of the supplier. To do this he had to wait until all the documents had gone through the system, then on the final checking he substituted credit

33

transfer documents bearing his own details and bank code. All the credit transfer slips were sent off except those for himself which he extracted, but the sheet showing the amounts to be transferred went to the company bank and were transferred to the suppliers' bank accounts, including those for himself.

By using this early system he ran a risk when he substituted the typed credit transfer slips, so he gradually worked on his system to cut to a minimum the risk of detection. The system he finally devised meant that he no longer had to rely on substitution and his false credit transfer slips were prepared for him within the normal system. The first part of the operation was exactly the same as his earlier system, but he now inserted his own details into two old and unused supplier's accounts. In this way when he made transfers by way of the amendments sheets the credit would go automatically to the account bearing his name and bank code. He had bank plates prepared with his own details on for impressing onto the already prepared credit transfer documents, but his name was made to look like that of a supplier. One account simply bore his own name with the addition of '& Son', whilst the second account also bore his own surname with the addition of '& Co'. He was now able to transfer credits direct into these two accounts by preparing false supporting documents which enabled all the transfer documents to be prepared. By this method he ensured that he had a regular and increasing supplement to his salary.

He still had some risks to take, however, because he had to retain the false supporting documents until after the money had been transferred to his own bank accounts. It was then a simple matter to destroy them. If there were any later checks made the folders for the two accounts would be empty. It was also necessary for him to retain the false supporting documents until after the very substantial cheque for the credit transfers was signed, and this had to be signed by two senior company officers. It was the usual procedure for it to be signed and delivered to the company bank on the last Friday of each calendar month.

A flaw

There is, however, a flaw in every fraud. The one which causes most difficulty for an internal fraudster is that he can very rarely afford to be away from his office, for any cause, as this is usually the time when a fraud comes to light. In this case the fraudster did manage to stay at work, or to make visits if he was on holiday, because he did not go away. In this way he was able to keep a constant watch on anything which might give him away. After four years of getting away with it he grew careless and decided it was time that he made use of some of his fraudulent gains. He and his wife decided that they would take a cruise for their summer holiday and made the appropriate booking. Unfortunately for him he left his wife to do the booking. She was unaware of the fact that he needed to be available on the last Friday of the month and booked a cruise which started on the last Saturday of the month and which started from a German port. This meant that they would have to leave for Germany at the latest on the morning of the last Friday of the month—before the cheque for the credit transfers had been signed, so he would not be able to destroy the false supporting documents. This caused the fraudster a problem, but he decided to go ahead with that month's fraudulent transfers. Instead of destroying the false supporting documents and the copies of the credit transfer slips he concealed them in his desk where he thought that they would be safe.

When he appeared before the court he used a plea of mitigation to allege that it was the fault of his employers who, he said, had treated him badly. He accused them of overlooking him for promotion and said that he had always been badly paid. He told the court that he had not used any of the stolen money but had paid it all back, the first large amount when he was confronted, and a second large amount during the course of the enquiry. Some of what he said may have been true, but the question arises that if he had been so badly paid, and if as he said he had paid back every stolen penny, where did he raise the cash to buy himself a business immediately he left court having received a suspended sentence?

Business fraud

A fraud conceived in the belief that it would save a company from liquidation was committed against a well-known company specialising in security equipment. The victim company had international contracts to supply security devices ranging from a simple lock to highly complex security doors. Originally, all orders were manufactured by the company's own factory, but time factors and manufacturing capacity had altered that.

Large numbers of orders were received because of their international reputation for reliability and many of their orders were put out to contract with smaller, but equally reliable, companies who were experts in their field and able to produce the goods to the same high standards. The company received an order from an overseas customer to supply two very complex and high-value security doors, which were to be produced, shipped to the customer, and fitted within a limited time. This order, which was to be the subject of the fraud, was placed with a sub-contracting company with the ability and know-how to produce the doors within the time limits set, and who were known to have previously met the high standard required. What was not known was at the time that the order was placed with the sub-contractors their company had serious cash flow difficulties, and were on the verge of liquidation.

The problem had been with them for some time, but in spite of an arrangement with their bankers in an effort to halt the inevitable collapse things were still going badly. The two directors were aware that if the company was forced into liquidation they would lose their homes which had been mortgaged by them to raise money to keep the company going. The order for the doors was sent to the sub-contractors in triplicate with the intention that one copy would be returned with the delivery note and doors, and the other with the invoice. The third copy was to be retained by the sub-contractors for their own records. It was this triplicate order form system which was to facilitate the fraud and cause the eventual downfall not only of the company but of the two directors as well.

Double payment

The two doors, although ordered as a pair, were made and delivered separately on different days to the security company, where they were to be packed ready for shipment to the overseas customer. Each door was accompanied by a delivery note, but only the first one was supported by a copy of the original order. The second door had only a delivery note with the order number typed on it. Eventually the sub-contractor sent two invoices, one for each door, quoting the delivery dates and the order number but seemingly with the price quoted on each invoice for a pair of doors. When the invoices were received a check was made to see whether or not the goods had been received, and in each case it was confirmed that a door had been delivered as stated on the invoice. At that stage no check was made on the price charged because this was the job of the invoice department. When they did their check no one spotted that each invoice was for the delivery of only *one* door with a price quoted for the *pair*, and the invoices were duly passed for payment. It was only some time later when the costing was being done for the invoice to be sent to the overseas customer that the apparent mistake came to light, and it was realised that the doors had been paid for twice.

At this stage, fraud was not suspected because the two directors of the sub-contracting company were believed to be honest and respectable businessmen and no one was aware of their financial difficulties. The overcharge was brought to the attention of the sub-contractors who at first denied that it had happened and commenced a series of delaying tactics, including suggesting that the mistake was in the price quoted when the order was placed. This gave them a little breathing space but eventually and reluctantly they were forced to admit that a mistake on their part might have occurred. They made no offer to repay the additional money received, and ignored the many requests for as long as they dared, but they were eventually forced to admit that their company was insolvent.

It was only at this stage that the security company learned that the sub-contracting company would have been forced into liquidation earlier had they not received the order for the doors. The directors of the sub-contracting company told the security company that they were unable to repay the overcharged amount, and suggested that the solution would be for the victim to take over the insolvent company as compensation. This might have been the answer to both problems, but during the course of the investigations into the viability of the suggestion certain other worrying factors came to light. It became more apparent that the overcharge for the doors was not quite the mistake it had been made out to be. Eventually, following other discoveries, it was decided by the victim that they had been defrauded and the police were informed and asked to carry out a criminal investigation. One of the objects of an investigation is, where possible, to recover stolen money or property but it was very quickly discovered that in this case it would not be possible as the two directors had used the money obtained by their fraud to pay off their own commitments to the bank in order to save their homes. Both directors were interviewed, and one of them made a full confession that the double invoicing was not just a mistake but a deliberate act of fraud. He said that it was an attempt to solve the company's problems, but when they realised that this was an impossible task they had decided to look after their own interests. The second director denied being responsible and maintained this attitude right up to the time of his trial when he then pleaded guilty.

It is usual in fraud cases for the criminal prosecution to take precedence over any civil proceedings, but in this case the losers, quite properly, wanted to make an effort to recover the very substantial loss as quickly as possible. They could have waited and relied on being awarded compensation by the court, or for a criminal bankruptcy order to be made on conviction of the accused. But they were aware that it was a rather forlorn hope that such a large sum would have been awarded by way of compensation. They were also aware that in bankruptcy proceedings they would also be unlikely to get even a small part of the money they had lost to fraud. Because the stolen money had not been used to prop up the ailing company but had been used by the two directors to pay off their personal debts, the victim company was advised to pursue a civil claim against the two men, even though the criminal enquiry was in progress.

The victim company followed this advice and commenced civil proceedings, but it will never be known what the outcome might have been. Before either the civil or criminal proceedings came to court the fraudsters both sold their homes and paid off the victim company. They probably did this in the hope that they could use this fact in mitigation at their trial, but they were both sent to prison. Their company was liquidated, and they both faced personal bankruptcy proceedings. Although the amount stolen in this case was quite high, it was categorised as minor fraud because it was a simple one-off situation, involving one company defrauding another company in a fairly simple way.

Not all matters of company insolvency and fraud are as simple and straightforward. Sometimes the decision to resort to fraud can involve a large number of people, some of whom are involved in the fraud at the outset, some who enter the fraud later of their own accord, and others who are dragged into it. Unravelling such a fraud can be a time-consuming and difficult task.

Collusion fraud

Fraud can affect almost anyone, even a small, solvent and happy business such as a small domestic coal delivery business which had been delivering coal to homes and small businesses in a city area since the days of the horse-drawn cart. Fraud reared its head when this small company expanded into a large company very quickly with a view to sale as a going concern. In this case they were not the victims but the perpetrators.

In the small business everyone, including the owner, was a worker: all were expected to take their turn at tipping bags of coal into cellars and coal bunkers. If left alone the business would have continued happily making a modest living for a number of people, just as it had in the days of the owner's father and grandfather. There would probably have been the occasional fraud on customers, committed by an unscrupulous delivery man simply overstating the number of bags of coal actually delivered. No one could have guessed at the extent of the fraud which was soon to overtake this small company.

A chance visit

It began with the chance visit to the company by a business entrepreneur who was in the area looking for business opportunities. He quickly identified the potential of this long-established small business. On his first visit he aroused the interest of the owner by explaining how easily the business could be expanded to bring in much larger profits. He had been quick to see that the company owned a very large wharf where the fuel for delivery to customers was stored, but that only a very small part of that wharf was used. There was plenty of room for much more fuel, and large areas for parking many more and bigger delivery lorries. The entrepreneur talked long and hard to the owner, and painted a very promising picture of the possibilities; the owner was impressed by what he was told.

The entrepreneur was allowed to carry out an examination of the existing business and he discovered that there were no contracts for delivery of fuel to such establishments as schools and larger factory premises, both of whom were large consumers, and where there was a need for such deliveries. The entrepreneur suggested that if he were allowed to become involved in the company he would have the contacts which would enable him to negotiate such contracts. The owner was further impressed by the talk of big profits from expansion which he was told would yield more profit per contract than the whole of the existing business. It was agreed that the entrepreneur would become involved in the business and as far as the contracts were concerned he was as good as his word. Very soon he had negotiated contracts with the various local education authorities to supply fuel to schools throughout a very wide area. He had also been able to negotiate contracts to supply fuel to many very large factory and business premises whose consumption was high. It was quite apparent that the small size and number of the existing local delivery lorries would be totally inadequate for the new and larger business, so larger delivery vehicles were bought and many new drivers were employed.

Contracts were also negotiated, via the Coal Board, with collieries for fuel to be collected and delivered direct to the schools and to business premises so that there was no need for it first to be delivered to the wharf. The dream which the entrepreneur had promised the owner soon appeared to be coming true. He was now the owner of a much larger business, the turnover was astronomic in comparison with his previous business and there seemed no reason why it should not go from strength to strength.

There were many things which should have caused concern to the owner, but he chose to ignore them. He was aware, but unconcerned by the fact that most of the contracts had been negotiated at very low delivery prices: he believed that the volume would make up for the low prices. He was, however, at that stage unaware that in some cases the fuel was being sold at about the same price as his company was paying for it. He was also unconcerned by the fact that his company had been committed to a very large hire purchase debt in order to buy the lorries necessary to deliver the fuel following collection from the collieries.

New directors

The entrepreneur suggested a new board of directors made up of some well-known people, including one titled, who would give the company prestige. This was agreed and the entreprenuer was able to nominate people who were willing to serve as directors without taking any active part in the company, being paid only a fee. All this served to build the company very quickly into a major fuel supply company, and the entrepreneur's intention was to sell it off as a going concern at a large profit before the real financial problems came home to roost. There were indeed very large financial commitments. It soon became apparent that it would be necessary to resort to fraud against the customers if they were to make the company pay its way and appear to be making a profit.

At first, this was done by simply inflating the fuel alleged to have been delivered to customers, particularly schools where there was no weighbridge to check the weight. The fuel was collected from a colliery where a delivery ticket was issued showing the tare (unloaded) weight of the lorry when it entered the colliery. It was weighed again when it left the colliery loaded and the gross weight was entered on the same ticket. These weights were entered on the tickets automatically at the weighbridge. The weight of fuel to be delivered was arrived at by deducting the tare from the gross weight. These figures would normally be entered on to a company delivery ticket which was left at the delivery point showing how much fuel had actually been delivered, and would be invoiced.

When fraud became necessary only some of the drivers were asked to be involved. They were told that if they would inflate the gross weight on the company delivery notes this would help the company by showing more fuel delivered than was actually on the lorry. Gradually all the drivers were recruited to become involved. They were rewarded by extra money in their pay packets. This was intended to be only a short-term measure. It was still the intention of the entrepreneur to sell off the company as a going concern and to get out with a very large profit for everyone.

The entrepreneur, however, had reckoned without the owner who now caused a very big problem. He had quickly got used to the idea of being the big man in a big business. He had no wish to relinquish his new-found status. In spite of all the entrepreneur could say or do he steadfastly refused to allow the business to be sold. It now became increasingly obvious to the entrepreneur that if they carried on as they were they would soon run into severe financial difficulties and it would be impossible to sell the business. He also realised that fraud had by now become so commonplace that almost every delivery was being inflated. The risk of the fraud being discovered grew daily. This was pointed out to the owner and the entrepreneur entreated him to sell the business and to get out whilst he was still on top. The owner was still determined to remain in charge.

Action needed

Something had to be done. The entrepreneur had no wish to become personally involved in the consequences of fraud. He was also worried that his nominated directors stood a chance of being embroiled in the consequences of discovery of the fraud, even though at this stage it was still comparatively small, and this seriously worried him. Eventually, he advised the new directors that there were some financial problems, and advised them to resign. He did not tell them about the fraudulent aspects of the business but they all resigned their directorships. The entrepreneur then arranged with the owner that he himself would leave the company on payment of a small fee. It was not what he had hoped for from the business but at least he would not now be involved in fraud.

The owner was left in charge of a new and expanded business, with large contracts to supply enormous quantities of fuel, but at prices which were impossible if the company was to survive. He also had large hire purchase debts for the new vehicles which had been bought, and a much larger staff with a consequent larger wages bill. At first he attempted to carry on using the fraud to inflate the weights of fuel delivered to schools, but he too soon realised that it would not be very long before he was caught if he did not think up some new ideas. The fraud and the business rolled on in the meantime and eventually all his staff, including the office staff, the outside staff, and the drivers were involved in this massive deception.

They were all being paid fairly high wages, plus an occasional handout, and therefore had personal reasons to keep the fraud going. The owner realised this and enlisted their help to think up better and safer ways to ensure that the company was profitable in spite of the low priced contracts. The suggestions came in thick and fast. One suggested method involved the delivery of a particular type of high grade fuel to a factory with no weighbridge. The fuel was of a type which could be supplied by only one colliery. The suggestion was that a lower grade of fuel would actually be delivered and that the higher grade fuel should be sold to another customer for its true value, but the colliery collection ticket would be used to support the delivery of the lower grade fuel.

At first the lower grade fuel mixed well with the higher grade already in the bunkers, but it would not be long before it was realised that something was wrong. In the meantime the customer paid several pounds per ton more for his fuel than it was actually worth, and the immediate risk of detection was much less than simply inflating the weight. Later, some deliveries were made of the genuine grade fuel to mix in with the lower grade stuff.

Other methods

Other methods had to be thought up and apparently quite by accident the weighbridge clerk at the company's fuel wharf discovered a fault in the weighbridge. Whenever a lorry entered the weighbridge it caused the needle to swing far over the actual weight of the lorry, and it was necessary to wait for the needle to return to the true weight of the lorry before the lever which recorded the weight could be pressed.

On this weighbridge they had recorded the weight of the postman and his bicycle at 10 tons. To do this needed good timing because the lever had to be pressed when the needle had reached its highest point and before it could start on its return journey to the correct weight. This was tried with lorries and they were able to record weights several tons in excess of the true weight of the lorry and its load. The discovery was put to good use. More fuel instead of being delivered direct to the customers was returned to the wharf. The lorry had its unloaded weight recorded on two weighbridge tickets before the driver left for the colliery to collect his load. When the driver returned with his load to the wharf he again passed over the weighbridge where his weighbridge ticket was stamped with the needle at its highest point recording that the lorry carried at least two tons more fuel than was actually there. It was then delivered to the customer as if it were the higher weight. When he was asked to become involved in this practice one of the drivers pointed out that if he was stopped and asked to go to a public weighbridge by a Weights and Measures Inspector the fraud would be discovered. To overcome this, the second weighbridge ticket, which had been recorded with the unloaded weight before the driver went to the colliery, was stamped with the true gross weight to be used only if the driver were stopped by a Weights and Measures Inspector.

Fraud factory

For well over a year after the entrepreneur had left, the fraud continued unabated with new tricks being thought up all the time. During this time the owner, who had only a modest life style when first visited by the entrepreneur, had moved to bigger and better things. His life style was now expensive, as was the running of his totally fraudulent business. His outgoings, both personal and business, were tremendous and it was not long before he ran into serious financial difficulties and was unable to pay his way.

He could not pay his suppliers but when he approached them for help they were impressed with his apparent performance and agreed to lend him the money to pay them. It was a very large sum and the suppliers took a floating charge against the company assets and the business and the fraud continued for a time. It was not too long, however, before the company was again in financial difficulties and this time the company was put into receivership.

At first the receivers could not understand how the business had been made to work but the fraud soon became obvious and a criminal enquiry was started. Twenty-four men stood in the dock at the Crown Court all accused of fraud and conspiracy, and twenty-three of them were from the fraudulent company. Twenty-one of those from the company pleaded guilty, and three, including the owner and one outsider, pleaded not guilty. The outsider was discharged by the judge part way through the trial, but the two from the company were convicted by the jury on overwhelming evidence after a very lengthy trial. Nineteen of those involved were sent to prison, including the owner and his managers, and the remaining four were very heavily fined. The judge, when passing sentence, described the business as a fraud factory. There was little left in the company for the receiver to handle and many people lost a lot of money.

Professional fraud

Many professional fraudsters are previously convicted persons and very often have also been made bankrupt at some time in their careers. After they have been arrested they will often apply for bail and, if it is granted, they will run new fraudulent ventures whilst awaiting trial for earlier frauds. It is not unknown for a group of fraudsters to have been committed for trial to several different crown courts.

The professional fraudster will almost certainly have some companies which he has formed and are lying dormant awaiting an opportunity to be used to commit fraud. The more experienced professional will form a company chain of ownership almost impossible to trace through, and will often be registered offshore in such places as the Isle of Man or some tax haven. Once they have been used for fraud the companies, having served their purpose, will be abandoned or liquidated.

The professional fraudsters, like ordinary businessmen in their legitimate businesses, meet people who are honest and have a special knowledge or skill or contact which the fraudsters know may be of use to them either at the time or in the future. If these skills or contacts cannot be used immediately a list of such people is made and kept until needed. Invariably, they are totally unaware of the fraudulent nature of the business, will not be informed of it, and will often not even become aware of it until they are totally committed, leaving them with a massive dilemma. When a new fraud opportunity turns up the fraudsters will look through their list of contacts to see if they have details of one or more with experience in the field where they intend to operate the new fraud. If they have they will recruit employees from this source. If possible the fraudsters will compromise their new employees in some way in order to ensure that they are unable to do anything about it when they discover that they are involved in a fraud.

On such group of fraudsters had been operating throughout the country for some time, liquidating and moving on when things got a bit hot. Although they were under investigation in many areas they had not been arrested. Having had to make a quick exit from one area they were looking for new opportunities when there was a miners' strike. A search of their records revealed that they had previously had contact with a man well known in the fuel and earth-moving equipment business. He was an honest man who had recently retired when they decided that the time had come to use him. The fraudsters already owned a company having a name which with simple alteration would be suitable for use as a business dealing in coal supply. They opened an office in a small Midlands town, near to the coalfields, with the intention of buying all available coal and selling it at a quick profit whilst demand was greater than supply because of the miners' strike. The profit from this fraud was not, however, to be made from simply buying and selling coal in the usual way, because that would mean that they would have to work hard to make a profit and would have considerable competition.

The fraudsters were experienced professionals who had operated many previous frauds. They knew that if they were to operate for only a short period they would be able to buy without actually having to pay many of their suppliers, and could therefore afford to buy at a higher price than their competitors. They would also be able to use transport supplied by companies who would not be paid, and keep as profit all the money paid to them by their customers.

Manager appointed

Immediately they had set up business their contact was approached, recruited and made manager of the new business. They then negotiated to buy coal at any price and sold it for whatever price they could get even if it was lower than the price they had bought it for. They were not going to pay for it anyway.

The fuel was moved from seller to buyer in hired transport, which meant that the fraudsters never had any physical dealings with the fuel: they simply built up debts for the hire of transport. If there was any argument with a transporter they simply moved to another company which was short of work because of the strike. They made excuses for the non-payment for fuel and transport because they knew that the end of the fraud would coincide with the end of the miners' strike, and they would be able to move on. They did pay some of their suppliers in part especially if they were able to supply more coal, but only if very pressed. Their new manager was able to introduce them to many small suppliers of coal, and to haulage contractors willing to provide transport, but he was kept in ignorance of the fact that the business was fraudulent.

To get him involved, they arranged for him both to rent business premises for them and to have telephones installed using his name in both cases. When the fraudsters visited the town they stayed in hotels booked by him with the bills sent to the fraudulent company. In this way he was both compromised and a future victim of the fraud. None of the money they received from their customers was actually paid to their new company. It was passed through channels to a holding company which ran a couple of legitimate businesses and was otherwise totally uninvolved in the fraud.

Professional fraudsters rely to a certain extent on an element of luck in any fraud venture and they found it in their introduction, by another contact from their list, to a man whom they immediately recognised as of a similar type to themselves. He was not as experienced as they were and when they listened to what he had to say they soon realised that he was trying to defraud them.

They were posing as London businessmen, in finance, who had a lot of money to invest, and who were looking for an opening in fuel supply. To the less-experienced fraudster they seemed to have been heaven-sent as he too had prepared for an opportunity to defraud someone. When he realised that there was a likelihood of a miners' strike he had bought an old colliery tip which he hoped would yield a lot of recovered fuel for sale at a good price. He could not believe his luck when he was introduced to what he saw as two 'London Mugs' with more money than sense. He realised that if he was careful he could negotiate the sale of the whole of his tip on the basis that it was all good quality fuel. He was completely deceived.

He signed a contract with them to supply 100,000 tons of fuel of a very high specification at a very high price. He knew that the tip in total weighed far more than the fuel he was required to supply, but in reality it was mostly reject coal with a very low value. Nevertheless, he went ahead and signed the contract in the belief that he would be able to deliver it without the buyers finding out that it was low quality until it was too late. They had hooked him by offering a very high price which was far above that which he could have expected even if he had been able to supply coal of the quality required by the contract. He was determined not to let the opportunity to make a killing slip through his fingers.

The contract he signed required the first loads of coal to be available for collection on transport hired by the buyer company immediately, the balance to be supplied within a specified period. During the negotiations the fraudsters had resold the whole of the 100,000 tons of coal to one buyer for delivery to their premises. The buyer was a very large concern dependent for their business on adequate supplies of coal of the quality which had been negotiated in the contract; inferior coal would soon clog up their furnaces. The owner of the tip had no access to fuel of the quality required by the contract. As there was a miners' strike he had little prospect of obtaining supplies but he was not concerned since he intended to make all the deliveries from his tip. The lorries which came to collect the coal were all hired transport. This suited the owner of the tip who knew the drivers would never question what was loaded on their lorries and he also knew that they were going direct to the customer's factory. When the coal was delivered the miners' strike was beginning to bite and because stocks were low it was put into immediate use, rather than, as the tip owner had hoped, being stored for future use. As expected, the furnaces quickly became clogged and the customer made an immediate complaint to the fraudsters. This was passed on to the owner of the tip who was reminded of his contract. He was told forthrightly that he must supply the remainder of the coal at the quality specified. The fraudsters knew that he would be unable to do this but they still sent their hired transport to the tip daily.

At first, the lorries were still loaded with coal from the tip but on arrival at their destination the loads were rejected. The drivers were then told to refuse to be loaded from the tip or anywhere else unless the coal was of the quality required by the contract. No fuel of the quality required was supplied and the delighted fraudsters sent daily invoices in respect of demurrage to the tip owner. This was to be their ticket out of the fraud because eventually the total for demurrage reached a quarter of a million pounds. The fraudsters then commenced civil proceedings against the tip owner. In the meantime, in spite of the strike, they continued to find coal to buy and sell, but they paid very few of their bills for the supply of coal, and none of their transport charges.

Eventually the miners' strike ended and coal became more readily available. The tip owner offered to supply coal of the correct quality for the contract but it was too late for him. The fraudsters refused and pressed ahead with their civil claim. Now that the strike was over the fraudsters owed a great deal of money for genuine coal supplied to them and this had been delivered to their customers who had paid them. They had also run up very high transport bills, none of which had been paid. The fraudsters' fuel company was put into liquidation with a large number of creditors, but these were more than covered by their only debtor, the tip owner, who owed a quarter of a million pounds for demurrage.

Their liabilities were about equal to their debtors and the money they had received in payment from their customers had been passed through a chain of companies to a holding company. It was now time for the fraudsters to move on, leaving their local contact to answer the irate suppliers and transport contractors, and with enormous personal debts incurred on behalf of the fraudulent company.

Gradually, the fraudsters' earlier activities caught up with them. By this time there were enquiries about their activities in all parts of the country where they had committed numerous frauds leaving many businesses in tatters. Although it was not possible to bring all their fraudulent activities to trial, there was sufficient evidence to convict all the team who, without exception, received fairly long prison sentences. After their sentences some of their other activities were investigated but very few trials ensued.

Where there was a trial they usually pleaded guilty and were given concurrent prison sentences, which meant that they served no longer in prison than the original terms imposed.

Fraud victims

Many frauds similar to the ones described will almost certainly be operating now. Many businessmen who have worked hard and believe themselves to be successful will be the unfortunate victims of the fraudster, from any of the categories mentioned. Unless these businessmen are lucky, or have very efficient fraud detection systems, they may end up losing everything and with the company in liquidation. In Chapter 6 the question of prevention and detection of fraud will be examined, and some guidance given on what can be done to prevent or minimise the incidence of fraud.

3   Major fraud

Definitions

Major fraud might be thought of in terms of the activities of
unscrupulous directors involved in multi-million pound mergers
and takeovers. Others, when considering the definition of fraud,
will think about those involved in insider share dealing yielding for
the participants many millions of pounds. The activities of such
people, however, are not as prevalent as might be thought and,
when discovered, are often fairly straightforward matters to investigate. The complications with such frauds usually lie in the law
involved, rather than the nature of the dealings. There are,
however, other frauds which are similar in style and execution to
minor fraud, which because of their extent or effect are considered
as major fraud. It is such frauds, rather than share dealings and
takeovers, which are most likely to affect an ordinary businessman
and these are the frauds examined in this chapter.

High-tech fraud

New or early technology can be a very fertile area to be used by the
unscrupulous to defraud unsuspecting victims. One such case
involved a clever technician who obtained large sums of money for
the development of his ideas and for the future sales of his product.
No one had actually seen anything other than a small box which
had the appearance of being part of a computer. No one had been
allowed to handle it or to see it work, although extravagant claims
had been made about its potential capacity.

All the technician really owned was an empty box, a vivid

imagination, and the ability to talk people into believing that he was a genius. What he said about the possibilities of his box were believed, because if what he said about it were true, it would revolutionise computers. It would be expedient for those involved in computer development to have access to it. On the technician's word alone many companies and individuals were prepared to risk money.

In the early 1960s laser and microwave technology had advanced considerably from its early days when it was proposed, in 1956, from theoretical work, that if the light generated by atoms after they had been excited could be organised to be given out at the same time and in the same direction, a very powerful new source of energy would be available. After several years of failure the first laser was made to work in 1960 and it was known as the 'ruby laser'. This was followed by other types giving a wider range of powers, colours, pulse lengths and continuous operation for use in a wide field of application. Although much research work was done in the United States, many companies in the United Kingdom formed departments with highly qualified technical people responsible for the development and production of laser and microwave devices. It was a very uncertain future for many of these people and then, as now, with computer technology, groups of people broke away from the big companies to work for themselves in this field.

One such group did this in 1966. They formed a partnership to start work in the design, manufacture and sale of laser systems. The partnership had much early success and within a year had 15 employees. Within two years, the partnership had become a limited liability company financed from money put up by the existing partners and some new directors. This was backed by a large investment from a merchant bank and by money from a major insurance company in the form of a debenture. Further financial aid was given by one of the big banks who agreed a very high level of overdraft.

Like many companies starting out on a new venture the group found that, in spite of everything, finance was tight. The directors, although highly skilled technically, were sadly lacking in management experience. They were also reluctant to accept the controls necessary to ensure the proper growth of the company. The senior member of the original team who was the brains behind the group's decision to break away on their own was determined to retain personal control of the new limited company as he had done when it was a partnership. This was particularly so on the financial side: he refused, in spite of advice, to appoint an accountant.

A similar group of people elsewhere in the country had been made redundant as the result of the closure by a large corporation of their laser research facility, and they too had formed their own partnership. They were invited to join the newly formed company. They agreed, but operated as a separate entity until early 1971 when all the UK operations were brought together under one roof. The new company was at first apparently very successful and attracted further investment from a European based company whose purpose was to invest in science-based companies with a good growth record and potential. They also formed a wholly owned sales company in Germany to increase sales in a growing export market throughout Europe.

In spite of all this expansion, the original leader continued to retain control of the book-keeping and accounting records. An employee of the investing European company who was an accountant had been appointed to the board of the UK laser company to look after their interests. He did not take part in the day-to-day business of the company. He had little or no access to the books and what little he did have was strictly controlled by the senior member of the original group. Other people were appointed with the express purpose of introducing a form of accounting and financial controls which would be acceptable to everyone concerned. Nevertheless, financial control remained firmly with the original senior member who was, by now, totally committed to a fraudulent course of conduct. By various means he was able to set the new appointees at each other's throats, resulting in resignations and accusations which kept them from looking too closely at what was really going on.

The first real opportunity to see that fraud was being committed came, but was not recognised, when the European investors agreed to double their investments but put in a proviso that the new investment would be made only if the profits for that year were in excess of figures which they set. Audited accounts were prepared and given to them.

The accounts did in fact show such a profit but were not accepted by the European investors until they had been examined by an independent firm of accountants. The accounts had been prepared on information provided by the senior member which had been unquestioned. The examining accountants in their review required an adjustment for goods which had been included in the year-end figures but which, although invoiced in December, had not apparently been delivered until January of the following year. This had the effect of reducing the profit figures below those required for the new investment. This setback proved to be the sort of luck which favours fraudsters. Everyone believed that because of the inclusion of this unfavourable account everything must have been genuine. Although the required profit figure had not been achieved the European investors felt that they were morally bound to assist the company and provided further capital on a temporary basis pending a refinancing plan, to be worked out. This was to cover the bank overdraft which had been exceeded in anticipation of the funds which were expected from Europe.

A good proposition

Up to this point the senior member had restricted his activities to falsifying the accounts in order to deceive debenture holders and investors and to cause them to increase their holdings in a company which was presented as an extremely good proposition. He did not hide the cash flow problems, but he now embarked on a secret course of deliberate deception and fraud to obtain money with which to keep the company going. He knew that if he were to make known the true state of the company he would almost certainly be forced into liquidation. He entered into leasing agreements with finance houses for equipment which did not exist; he entered into a factoring of invoices agreement with a finance company and used false invoices; he obtained money from his bank by drawing false bills of exchange in respect of goods allegedly sold and exported; he obtained finance from a leasing agreement in respect of goods required to be re-exported; he drew false promissory notes and obtained further money from the bank in respect of goods alleged to have been sold in Germany; he forged the signature of a German employee on a false bill of exchange in respect of fictitious goods allegedly sold in Germany (with dire consequences for the German employee despite her innocence); and he provided false information to the Department of Trade Export Credit Guarantee

Department which caused them to guarantee, and pay, large sums of money in respect of exported goods.

These moves were secret and will be described in more detail (*see* Simple methods, below). In the meantime the next overt act in this saga of deception would, if it had been successful, have given the company a foothold in the American market. There was in existence at this time a tariff barrier of 28 per cent in respect of goods exported to the United States. In order to try partly to overcome this a director of the company visited the US where discussions were held with a view to setting up a joint UK/US assembly facility. Whilst he was in the US the director learned that a company owned by a large US corportion was available for purchase. This company was the largest manufacturer of solid state lasers and laser systems in the world. The opportunity to purchase it appeared to be unique. The UK company was already the largest manufacturer of lasers and laser systems in Europe. The acquisition of the US company would not only make them the largest manufacturing company in the world, but would also remove the largest and only significant world competitor.

To acquire the US company very substantial additional funds would be needed, but an approach to the European investors aroused a great deal of interest. The company and the investors entered into negotiations but, as with the financial controls, these were conducted on behalf of the UK company entirely by the senior member. He was very persuasive and a proposed agreement was drawn up. The agreement required that capital would be raised by the issue of 46,000 £1 shares to be offered for sale at £5 per share and the balance raised by the company issuing an amount of 9 per cent loan stock in tranches of £50,000 at the beginning of each quarter. The European investors saw this as an opportunity to install proper financial controls. They insisted that they would not consider going through with any deal in the US, nor any refinancing proposals, unless these financial controls were installed and a financial controller appointed. The senior member agreed and a financial controller was appointed to work with the company. Once again the senior member was able to divert any interest which there might have been in the true financial state of the company. He did this by immediately plunging the financial controller into producing material in relation to forecasts concerning the UK/US merger to submit to the proposed financial backers. He pleaded lack of space at the company offices and the financial controller had to work mostly from his home, where he was able to have little to do with the everyday financial control of the company.

The storm clouds were by now gathering, and pressure was being brought to bear for the company to produce audited accounts and accountant certified accounts. The senior member, in order to meet this latest challenge, produced a draft balance sheet together with a draft profit and loss account which cleverly showed figures which were not in round thousands of pounds, giving the impression that they were genuine. At the same time he was bringing pressure to bear on the European investors over the proposed UK/US merger in the hope that he could get them to commit themselves financially to the merger so that he could use their money to pay off very pressing creditors.

The European investors were lulled, but not entirely satisfied, and they insisted on a board meeting to discuss the financial position of the company. The senior member once again came up to expectations and produced a new, but handwritten, draft balance sheet, together with a handwritten profit and loss account, for the board meeting, which showed the company to be in a favourable financial position. He also produced an estimated profit and loss account for the first nine months of the following year; an estimated consolidated balance sheet for the same period; and a forecast profit and loss account for the whole of the following year.

These painted a very healthy picture and were accepted by the majority of the board, but the investors still insisted that stringent financial controls should be introduced. They were totally unaware of the fact that all the figures used in these documents were false. The member of the board appointed on behalf of the European investors was not entirely satisfied and was instrumental in having a financial controller appointed; in the meantime, the European investors provided further temporary financial assistance. Some of the existing directors were so impressed by the figures produced by the senior member that they agreed to commit themselves to further financial investment in the company. But the bubble was about to burst. An investigation into the financial affairs of the company prompted by the director nominated by the European investors was set up and this time the senior member was unable to do anything to save the situation. In a matter of days it became apparent that the company was hopelessly insolvent, and a receiver manager was appointed. The fraudulent activities of the senior member came to light and a criminal investigation was started.

Simple methods

So what had been happening? The senior member, whilst lacking in management skills, had proved himself to be a highly competent swindler and forger. Although there is no evidence that he had any previous experience of fraud he had managed to keep the insolvent company going for many months by using fairly simple, well known methods. As far as the balance sheets were concerned he had overstated the debtors by a substantial amount, more than would normally be acceptable without question. Because he controlled the books and accounts he was able to bluff his way through and answer in one way or another the awkward questions. The enquiry quickly revealed that the company had not made any real profit for some time. If the debtors had not been overstated there would have been a constant and accumulating loss. He had been able to cover his fraudulent activities because accounts produced by reputable accountants were always based on figures which he had supplied. No actual books or accounts were ever produced to the accountants other than the false ones. False information in relation to sales and debtors permeated all the draft documents produced but this did not become apparent until after the collapse.

No fraudster would have been able to keep the company going by false balance sheets and false profit and loss accounts alone so it was necessary to look further to see what the senior member had been doing. It soon became obvious that he had, during the whole of the period that he was managing director, resorted to fraud and forgery in order to raise the necessary capital.

The investigation revealed that in one instance he had raised a substantial amount of money from a finance company by pretending that he had purchased a laser beam resister trimming station and needed help to buy it on hire purchase. He stage-managed this very carefully by setting up a test rig which he had received on loan from another company, and then pretended that it was the one he wished to purchase. When it became necessary to provide forms of idemnity by the other directors this produced no difficulties: he forged their signatures. His one difficulty was that the cheque in payment for the trimming station would be made out to the supplier and not his company. Even here he overcame the problem. By false stories and promises he deceived the managing director of another company into supplying false invoices for the components of the station, and then into exchanging the finance company cheque for one of their own. The finance company wanted audited accounts, but were satisfied with the same false ones he had prepared for the European investors. When the finance company representative came to examine the equipment to be financed he was shown the test rig supplied on loan. As the finance company representative later said, 'Who would really know what a laser beam resister trimming station should look like?'

The senior member obtained further substantial sums of money from other finance companies by using similar tactics. He forged signatures, pretended that machines had been sold to now non-existent companies and made up fictitious invoices. Even this was not enough. He needed still more money to keep the company going so he had to look elsewhere. His next victim was the Export Credits Guarantee Department of the Department of Trade and Industry. To assist exporters of high value goods the Export Guarantee Acts empower the ECGD, in consideration of the payment of a premium, to insure policy holders against loss resulting from sales to overseas customers. To holders of comprehensive guarantees additional facilities are available, whereby the ECGD gives a guarantee to a bank to repay finance provided by it to the exporter. This enables the exporter to draw a bill of exchange upon the bank and to receive in exchange the full value of the goods upon production of evidence of shipment of the goods. This gives the exporter three to six months' credit depending on the date of maturity of the bill, and whether the bill is accepted or not the ECGD is liable to pay the bank if the overseas customer fails to do so.

This was a ready-made source of fraudulent finance for the senior member, and an opportunity too good to miss for obtaining up to £40,000. Shortly after being granted the facility with a comprehensive guarantee by the ECGD, and the bank having agreed to advance the money, he forged a bill of exchange for £20,000 worth of goods allegedly sold to a customer in Holland. All goods sold by the company in Holland had to be sold through a Dutch agent who would receive the goods for onward transmission followed by the invoice. As the exporter had already received his money from the bank the agent would receive the bill for payment six months after the goods had been delivered. He would then be called upon to honour it. In this case there were no goods, merely a forged invoice given to the bank to support his claim on the bank for the value of the bill of exchange. No copy of the invoice was sent to the agent because the senior member had used an old invoice number which in reality related to the sale of two mirrors costing £45 which had already been sold to a Japanese company. He made out the invoice to show that he had sold £20,000 worth of laser equipment to the Dutch customer and indicated on the invoice that the goods had been delivered on a lorry whose registration number was recorded on the invoice.

It turned out that the registration number given as that of a lorry was the registration number of his own BMW car. On the copy of the invoice sent to the bank there was a forged signature for the receipt of the goods but as no documents were sent to the agent the fraud remained undetected. The agent first became aware that there was something wrong when he was presented with the bill of exchange for £20,000 for goods which he had never received and knew nothing about. There is little doubt that the fraudster had used this fraud to obtain money to keep his insolvent company going in the hope that within the six months before the bill of exchange matured he would have completed the financial agreement with the European investors. If this had been so he would then have been able to use the money from the investors to cover up his fraudulent activities.

There was another £20,000 available in this kitty and the fraudster made sure that he was able to use it by doing a similar thing in Germany. This time he used an innocent German employee from the German subsidiary who was tricked into opening a bank account in her own name in Germany in order to receive the bill for payment. He pretended that he was expecting a payment from Israel and told the German employee that it would cause difficulties if paid direct to the UK. He told her that the payment from Israel would be paid direct into her bank to meet the bill of exchange when it matured, and this would appear to be a sale made to a German company. Once she had passed him details of the bank account which she had opened he drew a bill of exchange for £20,000 using the German woman's name as if she were the company, then forged her acceptance on the bill of exchange. He once again used an old invoice number which in reality related to the sale of flash tubes to an English university, but altered to give the impression that it was for the sale of a laser station to a German company. He also forged the German woman's signature as having received the laser station.

By presenting the forged bill of exchange and the forged invoice to the bank he was once again able to obtain £20,000 to prop up his ailing company. The consequences to the woman he had deceived were quite distressing when the fraud came to light. The bill of exchange was presented for payment and she was called upon to honour it. Unfortunately for her no money had been deposited in her account as promised and she was therefore unable to meet it. In accordance with German law the only way she could escape paying the bill of exchange was by asserting, and proving, that her signature was false. This is a fairly lengthy and difficult process, and in the meantime the consequences of having to pay such a large bill of exchange hung over her. Because it was not paid the bill of exchange became the subject of a deed of protest, and as all bill protests are catalogued and passed to other credit institutes the lady was blacklisted. She was unable to obtain credit of any sort and this ban was extended to her husband. The fraudster was no help because he did not at that time acknowledge his fraudulent activities and he left the poor woman to sort out her problems alone.

Promissory notes

By this time, things were not going too well for the company and the fraudster resorted to every possible means to raise money to avoid liquidation. In addition to the bill of exchange facility there was a similar arrangement for promissory notes, but in this case the limit was set at the higher amount of £60,000. He used genuine business contacts and customers by forging invoices alleging that he had sold goods to them, and he was then able to draw forged promissory notes using up the whole of the £60,000 facility, all guaranteed by the ECGD. By these means he was able to raise a total of £100,000 but it was still insufficient to cover the needs of the company and his own ambitions.

Other methods of raising cash or credit needed to be devised whilst he awaited the investment from Europe. He scoured the advertisements offering company credit facilities and decided to try his luck with a finance company offering to assist companies financially by factoring invoices. He contacted, and eventually visited, the finance company where he presented a glowing picture of the future prospects of his company and they agreed to factor his invoices up to a maximum of £60,000. His entire dealings with the finance company were fraudulent from the start. He dealt with the whole thing himself and started by arranging to factor invoices which had in reality already been paid by the customers, but which he had redated.

He also used totally false invoices, again using invoice numbers from past sales of small items to various customers, redating them, and preparing them as if they were for the sale of high-value items. In order to allay any suspicions the finance company may have had in the early days of his fraud he made some payments in respect of the false invoices. The arrangement with the finance company was that all payments made by customers for invoices which had been factored should be paid, immediately upon receipt, into a trust account, and the credit of £60,000 could be kept at this amount by factoring new invoices. The payments he made were only token payments to keep the facility going until he had reached his limit of £60,000.

By this time the amount of fraudulent credit was quite substantial and far in excess of the £160,000 he had obtained from the bills of exchange, the promissory notes and the factored invoices. Only the investment by the European company could further postpone the inevitable discovery, but this was delayed longer than the fraudster anticipated, and people were becoming suspicious. In spite of his strong character, personality and ability to fend off unwanted enquiries, the end was in sight. A receiver would soon be appointed who would discover that it was not merely a case of business failure but that substantial fraud had been committed. The fraud had begun with the issue of false figures in balance sheets to attract investment, and ended when the fraudster needed to buy time for the investment and became entangled in a web of deceit and a series of criminal offences. By his deceptions he caused the downfall of his own company and serious loss to other companies: suspicion and accusations were levelled at innocent people, personal loss was suffered by many, including his friends and colleagues, and he had to stand trial accused of criminal offences. His trial was followed by a substantial prison sentence. He was made criminally bankrupt causing distress and hardship to his family.

Professional fraud

The professional fraudster never loses an opportunity to commit fraud. He often prepares well beforehand for the eventuality that something will turn up. It would be difficult to define the reasons why people become professional fraudsters, but there is little doubt that they enjoy preparing and executing very complicated intrigues and fraudulent business activities. If the same energies and expertise were devoted to legitimate business activities such people would quite probably become very successful. It seems, however, that for the professional, fraud is preferable to honest business even with its risks and consequences when caught.

Such a man was the professional fraudster who began life in very modest circumstances. At the outbreak of World War II he held a junior non-commissioned rank in the Territorial Army. He rose during the war years to the rank of colonel and for most of the war years did well for himself. Towards the end of the war, however, he fell from grace when his fraudulent activities were discovered and he was cashiered following a court martial. This, for him, was merely a temporary setback, because he had used his time in the army to learn a lot about people and about fraud. He was soon to put these lessons to use.

For several years following his discharge from the army he successfully practised fraud, mainly in foreign countries, until on one occasion he was just one jump ahead of the local police. He managed to get out of the country, and as they did not have an extradition treaty with the UK he was safe as long as he did not return. His hurried departure for home meant that he was unable to take away any of his ill-gotten gains, but he had to go quickly as he was aware that if he had been arrested he was likely to be imprisoned for a long time. He arrived back home with virtually nothing other than his fraudulent experience and know-how.

Dormant companies

Like all professional fraudsters he had prepared for such an eventuality: he had registered several companies which had either never traded or traded only briefly. These companies had then been allowed to lie dormant waiting for the right opportunity to be used for fraud. For a time the fraudster, having no capital, was obliged to work for a living. He used this period to make contacts and to renew credibility, all of which would be used eventually to commit the frauds which would yield the living standard to which he had by now become accustomed.

Although his companies had remained dormant he had maintained contact with his accountants who kept his companies ticking over although they did not trade. Only a few weeks before his fraud opportunity presented itself he had written to his accountants, in reply to their query, about one of his companies. He wrote: 'It is not contemplated that the company will trade in the foreseeable future and it has not traded for the previous five years.'.This was to become a significant fact in the enquiry after the fraud was discovered.

He did not really like working for a living, and he was looking for opportunities abroad in a country where his fraudulent bent was unknown. He had, during the time that he was working for a living, met a distinguished and upright Canadian citizen on whom he had lavished all his charm. As a result he settled on Canada as a suitable country in which to make his new start.

He had suitably impressed his new Canadian contact and had noted his details for future use. Once he had decided that Canada was the place for him he wrote to his Canadian contact and set out a very interesting story asking for assistance to get into Canada. As a result he was introduced, by letter, to another Canadian who had large business interests in Canada, with a view to joining that company. The Canadian businessman was looking for business openings in the UK. He was to become the fraudster's next victim. There was some correspondence, then the Canadian businessman visited London where he met the fraudster who turned on all the charm. He raised his old army rank and described all his fraudulent business activities as if they had been legitimate. The Canadian was very impressed. In the early days of their association it was still the fraudster's objective to use the Canadian businessman to facilitate his emigration to Canada and to provide him with employment. This did not seem to be going very well as there were no openings in Canada thought to be suitable for a man of the apparent calibre of the fraudster.

The fraudster had meanwhile learned of the Canadian's wish to open in business in the UK so he changed his plans. He decided that this could be the opportunity he was looking for to use one of his dormant companies. He wrote offering to help the Canadian to open a business in Britain and suggested that his own company could be the vehicle for their entry not only into Britain, but into the whole of Western Europe. He quickly built on the interest he engendered by this suggestion, mentioning in correspondence with his intended victim valuable political and government contracts both in the UK and Eire. He stated that his company was engaged in business consultancy with several ongoing lucrative contracts, and that its potential was very high. This could not have been true, as only weeks before he had written to his accountants telling them that the company had not traded for five years and was unlikely to do so in the foreseeable future. He contacted his accountants again, and this time told them that over the past two years he had revived his company and had several large contracts. He also embellished his real contact with the Canadian businessman and told his accountants that he was involved in talks with a view to the Canadian's taking a substantial interest in his business. There was no mention by either him or his accountants of the statement that he had not traded for five years. The fraudster asked his accountants to prepare audited accounts and provided them with a lot of false information for this purpose. He also asked them to increase the share capital from £250 to £10,000. To back up his story he gave the accountants a copy of a forged letter which purported to be from his financial director.

Glowing account

The original of this letter had been sent to the Canadian company. It gave a glowing account of alleged company achievements over the previous two years. The letter contained details of what purported to be the company's favourable trading position, saying that the main asset was invoiced receivables standing at a very substantial figure. Some years previously he had met a man who was an accountant and he had invited him to become a director of his company. He had refused but the fraudster had made a note of his details for future use. That time had now arrived but the fraudster discovered that the man had been living in the Far East for many years and would be difficult to contact. He countered by using the man's name to sign the letter giving him the title of financial director. The accountants who were to prepare the audited accounts saw no reason to question the information given to them by the fraudster and prepared a set of accounts based on the fraudster's information.

They were totally unaware of his previous fraudulent activities and did not know that his present course of conduct was also to be fraudulent. Having committed himself to his new fraud he decided to test the water by making an attempt to get money from his victim. He made a telephone call to his new contact in the Canadian company and told him that his own company had a cash flow problem, which whilst only temporary could cause the company to go into liquidation unless he obtained a substantial loan. He told his victim that his problem was caused by his customers who were slow to pay but that he had debtors who owed more than he sought to borrow. He also told him that he had a sure income of a similar amount to that which he sought to borrow, but committed for the next six months, and that even if all his debtors turned bad he would still break even. He gave him details of a contract which he alleged he had with the Eire government and which he said would shortly yield a profit of at least twice the amount he now sought to borrow.

The Canadian was not so easily convinced and in spite of everything that the fraudster told him he did not part with any money. The fraudster did not pursue the request too hard. He was content to have sown seeds of interest and did not wish to jeopardise the main intention which was to sell his fraudulent company to the Canadian victim. He changed his tactics and asked his intended victim if he could provide UK contacts where he might capitalise on his company's future. He was more successful with this move because the Canadian company's bankers had an office in Britain and the fraudster was given an introduction to the manager. Once again he turned on his charm and used his fraudulent expertise to paint a glowing picture of his company's prospects. He was so convincing that he was able to open an account with just £1, and was granted immediate overdraft facilities of £1,000 which he quickly used. He had, of course, to make the occasional deposit, but this presented little difficulty. He made most of his withdrawals from his new bank account in cash, then by soft talk and good stories he was able to talk other people into exchanging cheques for cash. He then deposited the cheques into the bank account as if they were payments from customers or clients.

Increased overdraft

During this time he built up in the mind of his new bank manager a picture of increasing and rewarding business and was believed to the extent that within two months he had been granted an increased overdraft facility of £2,500, which he exceeded by £1,500 without question. To him this was merely petty cash to be used as bait to catch the bigger fish; by inventing clients, and forging false contracts he soon had an agreed overdraft facility of £12,000. In the meantime he was setting the scene for the merger of the two companies.

When the victim visited Britain to undertake a serious exploration of the business potential in the UK and Western Europe and to take a closer look at the fraudster's company he was well looked after on the bank's money. There were no other real directors of the fraudster's company and very few genuine employees. The fraudster made sure that the victim did not meet anyone who would be able to say anything knowledgeable about the company. The victim had brought with him his financial controller/accountant with the intention that he should meet and talk with his opposite number in the fraudster's company—the man who had prepared all the financial information for the proposed merger.

The fraudster made arrangements for the meeting to be held at a place and on a date set by him but before the due date he forged a letter alleged to have been written by the financial controller of his company cancelling the meeting because of illness. This was sent to the Canadians at their hotel. As the date and time of the original meeting had been a few days before the Canadians were to return home there was no time to arrange a new meeting. Shortly after their return to Canada the fraudster wrote to them telling them that his financial director had died.

The fraudster had by now, however, done enough to convince the victim of his business success and integrity. When he returned to Canada he called a board meeting and recommended that his company should purchase the fraudster's United Kingdom company, with the name to be changed to one the same as the Canadian company but to include '(UK)' in the title. The purchase was agreed on the terms and conditions set out by the fraudster, who made an immediate visit to Canada where he made an impression on his new colleagues and business associates.

He was now in a better position to borrow money from his new Canadian associates, and did so at first in comparatively small amounts. With the bank, however, he was not so cautious and increased his borrowing considerably. He was appointed managing director of the UK company so was able to keep his finger on the pulse and stave off any enquiries which might have resulted in the discovery of fraudulent activities and his real intentions. In asking for a loan of £2,500 from the Canadian company to help over early financial difficulties he suggested that the best way to arrange the transfer was to pay the money into his own personal bank account because, he said, money transferred to the company would attract a five-year freeze on repayment of international loans. The victim, however, was quickly able to discover that this talk of a five-year freeze was not true and made a smaller loan of £1,500 to the company which was paid direct into the company account. He also arranged for a further £1,000 per month to be transferred to the UK company in order to secure their financial position. He believed that this would be returned from the monies which the fraudster had told him were due from clients. It is a sad fact of fraud that even when it becomes obvious to most other people that fraud is probably taking place the victim will often not see it. The Canadian victim was no exception. He slowly learned to exercise controls which led to the eventual downfall of the fraudster but in the meantime he allowed things to carry on in the hope that it would all come right in the end.

Forged contracts

It soon became obvious that the contracts about which the fruadster had told his victim did not exist but had been forged. This meant that the money which was expected to come into the company would not now be available. The fraudster was not slow to use everything and everyone he came into contact with. The so-called Irish contracts came into being when the fraudster met a visiting businessman from Eire who introduced him to the managing director of an Irish estate company. Without his permission, and without telling him, he made his Irish contact a director of the UK company and told the Irishman to whom he had been introduced that he had many clients who would be interested in setting up business in Eire.

He then told his contacts in Britain that he could arrange favourable terms if they would set up business in Eire. As a result of these contacts he was introduced to an Irish politician who was a member of the governing party in Eire. He forged agreements with almost every Irish company he came into contact with and also forged the signatures of the Irish politician and the Irish businessman on the contract acceptances. The Irish politician was genuinely interested in what the fraudster had to say and made arrangements for him to meet a business contact. This appointment was not kept, and in a letter to the fraudster the politician mentioned that he had been obliged to allocate the work to other businesses. This did not stop the fraudster from forging a contract with the same company for the distribution and marketing of the Irish products via an English company, whose directors were also unaware that their name was used. The only contact they had had with the fraudster was in connection with other matters which did not come to fruition. In his usual way he had obtained details of the directors and then used these in his false contracts.

In order to make his accounts more realistic the fraudstser even provided for doubtful debts. He did this by using his first Irish contact to make an agreement for him to carry out a study of the Irish company at no cost to them. It was the only genuine agreement he made and even bore the genuine signature of the Irish director.

But even in this agreement the fraudster was devious because he omitted to record the fact that the work was to be done at no cost to the Irish company. He did a little work and then sent survey reports to the company; he also sent invoices charging for the work done. Because the agreement had been that the work would be free the invoices were queried by the Irish businessman. He was told that these invoices need not be paid and were only for internal accounting and tax purposes. These debts were then included in his accounts as a provision for bad debts. There were many other so-called contracts in existence at the time the company was bought by the Canadians, but they were all forged, and there was not even one genuine business agreement or contract.

One more trick

The fraudster had one more trick up his sleeve. He asked people to carry out work for his company but was careful to select those who would have other commitments and were therefore unable to devote much time to his company's business. Some of the forged contracts were based on contacts that these people had made but which had not resulted in genuine work. At his trial he alleged that it was these people who had forged the contracts and caused his downfall. He suggested that they had devoted very little time to the work which he gave them. This last attempt, however, did not work. After a lengthy trial he was found guilty of many offences and sentenced to a long term of imprisonment.

Corruption

Not all frauds are committed by professional fraudsters, by employees, or by hard pressed businessmen on their own initiative.

There is always present the spectre of corruption which, once introduced, can creep insidiously through any organisation. The result of this corruption can often be a fraud of massive proportions. Corruption will often start with what is regarded as normal business entertainment, such as an invitation to lunch or dinner. Before long the person who is being entertained probably accepts gifts and is then deeply committed. It is at this point that the corrupter usually strikes. He may at first suggest that the victim performs a small task for him just as a favour, but before very long the corrupted employee is committing acts which are fraudulent and against his employer's interests. If not discovered at this stage the corrupting influence can spread to other employees who will also become involved, until finally there is a large fraudulent conspiracy operating.

False invoice

A well-known and very large company was the subject of a fraud enquiry which, like a lot of such enquiries, started with the discovery of an invoice which seemed to be wrong. An internal check revealed several more similar unexplained invoices, all from the same supplier, and as they appeared to be false the police were informed and they opened a criminal enquiry. At first it appeared to be a small fraud involving one supplier and one employee, but as time went on the enquiry got bigger, involving other employees and suppliers, and a substantial sum of money. The company directors decided that they would have all documents checked for a particular period, with the result that in addition to the fraud they discovered that large quantities of components were being ordered but were being delivered to an address which was not their own premises. This led to another major enquiry and the discovery that some employees were running their own company, supplying components to others, and even had an export market. All their supplies were of course paid for by the victim company.

It did not end there. When the supplier was arrested and his books and documents seized there was amongst them a diary which contained the names, at particular dates, of employees not only of the victim company but of other companies in a similar line of business. A check of these names showed that they were all employed in the purchases departments of their respective companies, some in senior posts. Linked with these names on the same dates were the names of other suppliers to these companies. The investigation revealed that on the dates on which names were entered there were also the names of restaurants and hotels where there had been meetings between the named persons. It soon became apparent that the suspect company must have had a massive entertainment bill from the number of people who had been wined and dined and it later transpired that the employees had all been given expensive gifts.

These gifts were made mainly by the one supplier whose diary had been seized but on some occasions gifts had been made by other suppliers. It became clear that here was an elaborate web of corruption which had started with the corruption of one employee and spread quickly to other employees and other companies. Most of the approaches were made by the corrupt supplier but some employees were brought into the conspiracy by the earlier corrupted employees. They in turn approached other suppliers to provide gifts in exchange for favours. Some of the employees were in such positions that they were able to dispense with a supplier who would not conform and they were able to use this as a threat. Not all suppliers were corrupt, but there were sufficient to give the employees involved a life style very much above that which they could enjoy from their earnings.

Net of corruption

In exchange for lavish entertainment and expensive gifts the corrupt employees were expected to pass for payment invoices which were grossly inflated either as to the quantity delivered, or at a much higher price than would ordinarily be paid. The net of corruption became so widespread that the fraud was able to continue for a long time, causing an enormous loss to the victim companies. There were several large companies involved as victims and all except one asked for police enquiries. It was revealed that many emloyees from each of the companies had been corrupted, and many others who were innocent were dragged into the enquiry through no fault of their own. Some of these innocent people had unknowingly been used to assist in passing invoices and were therefore involved in the fraud and needed to prove their innocence.

One of the victim companies, which had suffered from fraud in the past, introduced very exacting conditions to ensure that companies who wished to be included in the approved list of suppliers were suitable. One condition was that the factory premises of the supplier had to be visited by a senior employee nominated by the company who would ensure that they had the capability to manufacture the required items. This presented no problem for the fraudulent suppliers even though they were to have their factory premises inspected by uncorrupted personnel. The items they had contracted to supply were not made by them but by another manufacturer who was not on the list of suppliers. They simply bought from him and then delivered to the company as if they had themselves been the manufacturers. When they were to be inspected they borrowed the factory premises of the non-listed supplier and invited the company to send their inspector. They even went to the lengths of having a large sign made which was put up at the factory to be inspected covering the true name of the company owning the premises.

The fact that the address was not that of the supplier was also no problem for them because immediately they were listed suppliers their corrupted contacts merely altered the address for payment in their own records. The only deception the real manufacturer of the items was involved in was over the premises and he sold the items to his contact at proper competitive prices. The supplier to the company, however, delivered the goods to the victim company and sent grossly inflated invoices for the attention of the corrupted employees. As time went on and the gifts to the employees became bigger so did the cost of items supplied. At the time of discovery of the fraud many items were being supplied at about one hundred times their true value.

The final cost of this web of corruption, conspiracy and fraud will never be known. The losses to the victim companies were substantial not only from the fraud itself but also because it was necessary to examine many millions of invoices and other documents. Employees who should have been involved in their ordinary daily business were diverted to assist and they also had to dismiss many key personnel who were amongst those corrupted. They learned a lot about their inadequate systems and have now installed more secure systems and checks, but the cost was still enormous. The one company which did not allow a police enquiry sacked all those they believed to have been involved in the fraud, but it is a sad fact that they have been the subject of fraud against their company in the past, and will almost certainly be victims again. For the fraudsters who were caught, both suppliers and employees, there were in most cases prison sentences, fines and criminal bankruptcy orders. Most of the gifts which had been given were confiscated and many of those involved are now unemployed and, often, unemployable.

Contract fraud

While the purchases department of a company may, on occasion, be a breeding ground for fraud and corruption there are other areas where fraud will develop. One of the most likely is where contracts are involved. It has often been said that in many foreign countries there is a policy, sometimes official, whereby a large payment is required in order to secure a contract. In Britain and many other Western European countries the practice is not only discouraged but is a criminal offence. However, where contracts are sufficiently large the competition to win them will sometimes involve corruption and fraud. The measures taken to ensure fairness in the tendering and awarding of the contract are usually extensive, but for the fraudster intent on beating the system they are not insurmountable. Where a project which is to be put out for tender is sufficiently complicated it is often difficult to make it totally secure. This will be exploited by a determined candidate who is not averse to fraud and corruption.

Very often a company which does its business by tendering for contracts will make its first move into the field of fraud and corruption quite unintentionally. This can happen because they have employed a person who has the desire to be successful at any cost. Once he has used corruption the company will often find it difficult to reverse the process and may well become themselves knowingly involved. A successful corrupter usually has the same abilities to convince as the professional fraudster and will use them on those to be corrupted and on his own colleagues.

The victim of such a person was a very large European organisation which expanded its empire to England and formed a totally English-run company to seek contracts in Britain. At first this was moderately successful and the directors decided to expand their UK operations. They sought the services of a man with an international reputation for success in winning contracts, and who had spent many years in this line of business in the Middle East. He had not been with the company very long before they were successful in winning several very large contracts; they had also

71

been required at the request of their new man to make payments to various people. They did not ask too many questions and were probably aware, and ignored the fact, that the payments were corrupt payments to key personnel of the company awarding the contract.

Mild protests

Some of the senior people in the English company did make mild protest, but before long pressures were brought to bear by the European parent company for the English directors and senior employees to co-operate with the apparently successful new man.

Soon these same directors and senior personnel, as well as the European parent company, were themselves irretrievably involved in the intrigues of fraud and corruption. The new and successful addition to the company was made a director of the English company. He based his success on the fact that, at his company's expense, he earned himself a reputation as a very generous person. He not only wined and dined those about to be corrupted, but would lay on hospitality and expensive entertainment for large groups of people from the companies who had contracts to award. He arranged transport for groups of people to visit night clubs and at the end of the evening, following dinner, they would all receive a small gift. Those selected for corruption would often receive a more substantial gift. Sometimes he would seek out people who might later be useful to him and give them gifts. During the enquiry into this fraud it was found that several employees of some companies had been given substantial gifts but had been uninvolved in the actual fraud.

The fraudster also sought out for corruption employees who would not be involved in the actual awarding of the contracts but would afterwards be involved in administering it, once awarded.

First it was necessary to win the contract. It would have been easy simply to put in a very low bid and hope for the best, but this would probably attract attention and questions. The first area of operation insofar as the new contracts director was concerned was to get at the people involved in the technical aspect of the contract, and to this end he would select people in this field as targets and, where possible, lavish them with gifts so that they became corrupted.

It often happens where a contract is sufficiently complicated technically that after the closing date for tenders to be submitted, and before the actual award of the contract, all tenders received will be passed to a technical group for study. This is to ensure that they conform with the requirements. If they do they are returned with a report from the technical department for the contract to be awarded to the tenderer who meets the technical requirements at the best price. It was at this stage of the process that the contracts director was able to get at the employee he needed to ensure that he won the contract. He arranged with the contact he had made in the technical department that when the tenders were received by them for checking they would be made available to him for his own checks.

The contact was a man in a sufficiently high position to give him access to the premises without being checked and this enabled him to leave the factory in the evening with all the tenders in the boot of his car. Arrangements had been made by the contracts director to have them all copied at his own premises so that they could be returned by the contact to the factory the following morning and no-one else knew that they had left the premises. In this way the contracts manager of the corrupt company was able to study his competitors' tenders, then substitute new technical details or a new price, which he handed to his contact to be inserted in his tender before they were returned for the contract to be awarded.

The contracts thus obtained would often run into millions of pounds and be well worth winning if they were awarded at the right price. Not all the contracts won this way would have paid a profit, however, unless there was some other fraudulent means of ensuring that they did, and also ensuring that the profit covered any of the substantial payments made corruptly to the employees.

Budget price

The type of contract usually sought by this company was one with a very high contract value, where the customer had almost certainly decided on a budget price for the project before asking for tenders. The budget price was usually much higher than the price expected in the tenders, but once set it was not altered. Even if the tender accepted was well below budget the whole of the money would be available for the project if needed. This was a fact well known to the contracts director and he also knew that it was common practice to use any surplus balance from the budget to cover contingency payments. As well as corrupting the technical man who could give him access to the tenders he also corrupted employees who would be responsible for passing items for payment from the contingency part of the budget. In this way he was able to submit a low tender which would ensure that he would get the contract, but was also in a position to manipulate the balance of the budget as contingency payments and thus boost the true value of the contract.

The contingency fund also served as a source of money for corrupt payments. Some parts of the contracts would require specialist work which the contracting company could not itself do and therefore would need to sub-contract. For this purpose the contracts director usually used small companies on whom he could impose conditions not normally acceptable. In one instance he obtained £50,000 by forming an offshore based company and arranged to send an invoice for this amount to a sub-contractor. The sub-contractor would pay the invoice then pass on the charge to the main contractor alleging that it was for materials supplied and work done. The contractors in their turn would include this same amount as a charge against contingency and it would be passed for payment by a corrupted employee. In this way the contracts director had £50,000 to use for corrupt payments which had been unknowingly supplied by the customer. Some of the money obtained in this way would also be used to pay for the lavish entertainments and gifts, and would not always be paid direct to a corrupt employee. Where corrupt payments were made, however, especially if they were for large sums, they were usually made into foreign bank accounts. The corrupted employee was then invited to take a holiday in the appropriate country so that he could collect the money.

Numbered or strangely named Swiss accounts were not uncommon in this fraud, and payments into them were made from a variety of sources including the offices of the parent company in Europe. But even the cleverest of fraudsters makes mistakes and the contracts manager was no exception. His mistake was to disgruntle one of his own key employees who was not corrupt but was used to do some of the work on the illegally obtained tenders. Not only was he disgruntled but when he complained to management he was dismissed. What was not known was that he had kept copies of all the work he suspected of being false and had made extensive notes on the activities of the various directors and senior employees involved in the fraud, and in particular of the activities of the contracts director. He made full use of his notes and knowledge and once matters were out in the open the majority of the directors who had been dragged unwillingly into the fraud confessed their part. Most of the corrupted personnel from the victim companies were identified and at the conclusion of the enquiry many of them went to prison. The victim companies overhauled their systems of awarding contracts, but their losses were heavy.

4   Common fraud

Arson

There are many types of fraud, including arson, which are quite common in that they can be categorized, and are committed fairly often. Fire is a formidable weapon in the hands of a fraudster because it has its own fascination and fear and is so destructive that it can often destroy the evidence needed to prove fraud. Thoughts of fire conjure up in some people the pleasurable and welcoming glow from the hearth on a cold night. For others fire conjures up the fascination and horror of a major catastrophe with the fire brigade in action and people dying. But to the fraudster it conjures up the hope of turning a loss-making enterprise into a profit.

Non-accidental fires are not all started by those who use fire to cover up a crime, such as the murderer who burns the body, the political fire raiser or the businessman who burns down his loss-making warehouse and who has the clearest and most easily understood motive. There are those who kill themselves by burning, those whose motive is simply revenge, such as the disgruntled employee who burns down the factory, or the jilted lover who sets fire to the usurper's or ex-lover's property, or even the fire raising vandal.

It is a disquieting fact that the yearly figure for reported cases of arson, which includes fraud, increased by 350 per cent in the last ten years; and the true picture may be even worse. The chief general manager of an insurance company recently reported that more than half the major fires in Britain are the result of arson. That, he pointed out, compared with about a third of major fires resulting from arson a few years ago. The manager blamed 'declining social standards' for this situation. But nothing is new: the insurance company itself was founded nearly 200 years ago as a mutual fire office to issue policies of insurance against loss or damage by fire, because, said the founder, 'it is calculated to lessen calamity, to prevent imposition and to remove the temptation there is for evil-disposed persons to destroy property, first having insured it.'

The nature of the crime of arson makes it extremely difficult to recognise. It is not always obvious that a crime has been committed or that the fire was not an accident, and this can often never be properly determined. It is recognised that the investigation into the cause of fires is a complex science which relies heavily on experience, common sense and powers of deduction. An investigation into a suspect fire relies heavily on the forensic scientists, who are usually called in by the police or the fire brigade's Investigation Unit, but trends are often a pointer. A few years ago premises in the 'rag trade' were particularly prone to non-accidental fire; this was followed by printing premises, and now the indication is towards large warehouses.

Arson as a means of fraud makes itself attractive because it is often almost impossible to locate jemmy marks on a window frame if all the doors and windows have been struck by a fireman's axe. Flooding a premises with water does little to assist the search for clues. This creates problems not only in the destruction or contamination of potential forensic evidence but collapsed buildings or fire-damaged property makes examination difficult. The fraudulent arsonist, however, does not always get it all his own way because fire can be fickle and fail to destroy all that the arsonist has set up. Fire investigators and forensic scientists are often able to locate the precise point at which ignition took place, or the areas in which the fire has been burning for the greatest length of time. This is possible even if objects such as furniture have been misplaced, disturbed or removed prior to the fire being started. Once it has been determined *where* a fire started it often becomes quite apparent *how* it started. This, combined with other evidence, such as the removal of goods from a warehouse, or more valuable items of equipment from an office, will often reveal a criminal arson.

Change of routine

Perpetrators of fires who seek to gain financially are perhaps the most difficult to guard against. The arsonist will probably have planned the fire and evidence of the pre-meditated crime may be apparent. This may not only lie in the physical evidence extant but also in any change of circumstance or routine involving the perpetrator which occurred immediately prior to the fire. For example, the unusual removal of pets, or the removal of such things as cylinders of gas which might cause an explosion and injury which the arsonist does not seek. These can be pointers to the fact that the fire was non-accidental, and is probably arson.

Arson for the purposes of fraud is often committed with the intention of claiming against an insurance policy. This is not always successful, even where there is no direct evidence of arson but only a strong suspicion. A person who committed arson with such an intention was a manufacturing jeweller who claimed the loss of his premises and all his stock. His claim was avoided by the underwriters on the grounds of non-disclosure of material information when it emerged that he had at least one conviction for handling stolen property. The position is that where a fire leading to the loss or destruction of property takes place by the wilful act of the insured person himself, or someone acting with the insured person's privity or consent, then the cause of the fire becomes immaterial. This conduct, coupled with the making of a claim on the insurers, constitutes a fraud. It has even been the case that where a person altering the structure of his property is so careless that it results in the complete destruction of that property, the person, whilst not fraudulent, has no claim on his insurers. Such a claimant was told that his policy did not include the risk of stupidity.

It is not unknown for someone to buy out an ailing business with the express intent of burning it down in order to make a fraudulent claim against their insurers. Such a case was that of the two London barrow boys who bought a drapery business in a southern coastal town. It had been a business of high repute, run successfully for some years by the previous owners. Within a month of the acquisition of the business the sum insured on the stock against the risk of fire had been increased by about 500 per cent. Within one month of the increase, on a Saturday evening at around 6 pm, after the business had closed for the day, an elderly lady who lived above a shop on the opposite side of the road to the drapery business saw one of the two new owners re-enter the shop with a can which she described as one which she would have expected to contain petrol or paraffin. She saw him leave the shop again within a short time carrying the can, and some 15 to 20 minutes later the building went up in flames.

The elderly lady, who had been watching these events with

interest, telephoned the police and the fire brigade. By this time the two new owners were hot footing it back to London by road, but as a result of the elderly witness's actions were arrested before they had got too far away, and were brought back to face the consequences. They were tried and found guilty of arson and fraud. Counsel for one of the accused decided in mitigation to bring to the attention of the judge the fact that his client was not of very high intelligence and said: 'M'Lud, my client is not a man of very considerable intelligence, not the kind of man who would set the Thames on fire....' At this point the judge intervened and said: 'Mr Defence Counsel, I'm inclined to agree with your comments, unless, of course, he had insured it first.'

Charity fraud

While fraud evokes feelings of fear and fascination, charity invokes feelings of compassion and wanting to help. Collecting money for charity in Britain is booming and can often yield vast sums of money for very worthy causes. Take, for example, the recent efforts of the pop world which raised many millions of pounds for famine relief in Africa; the television personalities who launch projects for particular causes raising similar sums; or Oxfam which quietly and consistently raises vast sums of money for foreign aid.

There are many examples of good work ensuing from the hard work of dedicated people, but not all money allegedly raised in the name of chairty is really intended for that purpose. There is evidence that there is a disturbing growth in charity-related fraud and abuse, giving tax privileges, rate relief and grants.

For a group to enter this booming charity business it is necessary to register with the Charity Commissioners. This, in theory, enables the Commissioners to exercise controls, but in practice it means only that they have determined at the outset that the organisation's stated purposes are exclusively charitable at law. In some cases the Commissioners have no further contact with a charity from the day it is registered. It is not even possible at times to check on whether or not the bona fides of any charity have been approved. Investigation of charity-related fraud is hampered by the lack of proper accounting procedures, and many fraudulent charity collections merely move their area of operation if investigated. Charity is an area of rich pickings for the fraudster who will have no real compassion for the afflicted or underprivileged, but will use them for his own ends. Most of us have encountered the door-to-door salesman who asks us to buy inferior good at inflated prices on the promise that the majority of the proceeds will go to a charitable cause, or that the goods on sale were made by and are sold on behalf of handicapped people. The people who commit such frauds will very rarely accept that they are defrauding not only those who give in the belief that they are helping less fortunate people, but that they are also defrauding these same less fortunate people. Charity is a worthy cause, but there are those who believe that charity begins at home and live very comfortable lives on the proceeds.

In an investigation into the activities of a man who was raising money on the grounds that it was going to support a hospital, a visit to the hospital revealed that he was in truth donating money to them. When the amount of money received by the hospital was checked against the totals collected it was found that they were receiving only two pence from every pound raised. This was pointed out to the hospital authorities who said that while they would have liked it to be more they could offer no assistance to the enquiry because if they helped to stop this man raising money they would then get nothing. A little, in their opinion, was better than nothing. This, unfortunately, is the attitude adopted by many organisations who rely on charitable donations for their existence.

Charity has very few watchdogs and the large and increasing number of organisations makes the job of the Commissioners very difficult. The bogus or fraudulent collector has very low moral values, and the large amounts of money to be made dull his conscience. As long as there is want there will be charity, and as long as there is charity there will be charity fraudsters.

Advance fee fraud

The fraudster who bases himself in a foreign country but commits his frauds in the UK is not uncommon because the fraudster knows that this makes any enquiries by the victim or the police more difficult. Fraudsters who commonly do this are those who operate advance fee frauds by pretending that they are able to arrange large business loans. Many businessmen have times when they find it necessary to seek more capital either to expand their business or to diversify, and they will seek the money they need at the most advantageous terms. This can often leave them wide open to the fraudster whose method of making his living is to pretend that he is capable of making arrangements for large overseas loans on the payment of fees in advance.

The advance fee fraudster will usually have some business connections in a foreign country, preferably one with a good economy, and even more preferably a long way from the UK. It may be that he has legitimate business dealings in the foreign country and may well have an ongoing company based there, but it is usually a company specifically set up for the purposes of his fraudulent activities. He will usually have impressive letter headings listing directors and associates, and will have corresponded with major business and banking houses in that country merely to obtain their letter headings. He can then forge letters which will be used to impress his potential victim. Not all his letters will be forged: he will probably have made approaches to these same businesses in the foreign country and put hypothetical propositions to them merely to possess a reply which can also be used to impress his potential victim.

Whilst in Britain he will seek out people who are looking for capital investment or a large loan for their business. He will impress them with his foreign contacts and lead them to believe that he has access to large sums of money available for investment or loan. He may pretend that he is an agent for a large foreign business organisation and that he has authority from them to seek opportunities for their investment in the UK. He will produce his forged letters, using the genuine letter headings, to back up his claims. By this method he will gain the confidence of his victim and will then ask for very large fees. Once these fees have been agreed the fraudster will ask for them to be paid in advance of the loan being approved and will then go back to the foreign country probably never to be seen again by the victim. If the fees are not immediately forthcoming the fraudster may well forge other letters from the alleged investor stating that the money for investment has been deposited to his order and he will then demand his fees before he will release the money. There will of course be no money deposited and once he has the fees safely in his possession he will then return to the foreign country. He will endeavour to keep his victim at bay for as long as possible by inventing difficulties. He may even ask for more fees. Occasionally this is successful, but eventually he will no longer be available either in Britain or at his foreign business address which will either remain dormant or go into liquidation.

Life insurance fraud

Fraudulent life insurance policies are almost as old as life insurance itself. There have always been people who will seek to defraud their insurance company after having taken out life insurance policies. The usual method is that the insured person will mysteriously disappear, probably leaving a pile of clothes on a beach or river bank. They will almost certainly have prepared the ground beforehand to ensure that their clothes are found and that they are quickly presumed to have died. Quite often, but not always, their dependent relatives will be involved in the conspiracy and will seek payment of the insurance policies. If they are involved, they will almost certainly also disappear following the payment of the policies, but if not they may well hear from the 'dead' person once they are safely in possession of the insurance money.

With travel to other countries being easy, and with the large influx of people from other countries who now live and work in the UK, the opportunity for this type of fraud has increased considerably. It is not uncommon for a foreigner living and working in Britain to make a lone visit to his home country, and to 'die' there, leaving his grieving widow to collect the insurance money. She will almost certainly be in possession of a death certificate and will have retained the services of a solicitor, and probably a friend of the same nationality who claims to have been present when the husband died. After collecting the insurance money the widow will decide to return to her own country where her husband will be miraculously resurrected.

In a recent case, the potential defrauder approached an insurance broker and asked him to arrange high-return life insurance policies with several companies. The policies were issued by at least five insurance companies, and the total amount of insurance on this man's life was in the region of £500,000, with the first year's premiums paid in advance. Shortly after taking out these policies he decided to pay a visit to his home country with a friend from the same village, but left his wife and many children in Britain. Before his departure he put all his affairs into the hands of a solicitor because he said that he intended to be away for a few months. The family friend who had accompanied the insured man on his home visit returned alone some weeks later and brought with him a death certificate which said that the insured man had been drowned in a river accident. The widow was only too happy to let him take charge of her affairs and he made visits to the solicitor who was instructed to make claims on the insurance policies. He did not immediately do this, but he did write to each insurance company asking for details of the policies and the amount which would be due in each case.

Chance meeting

The broker who had placed the policies for the allegedly dead man had also known him for some years, and on a visit to one of the insurance companies to check on his commissions for other policies he was surprised to hear of the death of his client and the fact that claims were to be made. He was surprised because on a visit to Germany only three weeks before he had seen the same man very much alive and well. He had not spoken to him but he was quite sure that it was the same man. He alerted the insurance company to this fact, and they in turn wrote to the 'dead' man's solicitor telling him of the meeting in Germany. Fortunately, as no actual claim had yet been made, none of the insurance companies had paid out on the policies. They informed the solicitor that payment would be suspended while further enquiries were made. The friend of the 'dead' man and his 'widow', via their solicitor, protested quite strongly about this but the insurance companies still withheld payment pending enquiries.

The five insurance companies who had issued policies joined forces and sent an investigator to the 'dead' man's home country to make enquiries as they were now quite sure that the death certificate was a forgery. The investigator learned a lot from his visit and discovered that there was a local market in forged death certificates, but he could not find any actual proof that the man had not died as stated on his death certificate. There was a wall of silence in the area, and threats were issued to anyone who attempted to help the investigator. The investigator returned and made his report, which was not really sufficient to delay payment of the policies for much longer.

There was, however, an unexpected sequel to the investigator's enquiries in that shortly after he had returned to England a letter was received by the English police written on behalf of the 'dead' man. It stated that he was still alive, that he was still in his home country and destitute; it alleged that he was the victim of a conspiracy, and he offered to return to Britain to give evidence if someone would pay his fare. The insurance companies were very pleased with this unexpected result, and the man did eventually return to England where he and his friend were tried for and convicted of fraud. Ironically enough the man had never been in Germany: the broker had made a mistake when he said that he had seen him there. It was, however, the sort of lucky break that all victims of fraud need and in this case it saved the insurance companies a total of £500,000.

This man very nearly got away with his fraud, but not all of them are as well thought out. At about the same time another man from the same country also 'died' whilst on a lone visit home, and his death certificate said that he had died after falling from a ladder when repairing the roof of his father's house. He too had taken out large insurance policies with several insurance companies, each of which received a claim, but each giving a different version of the death. The insurance companies quite naturally refused to pay up on the policies and the 'dead' man, upon learning of this, became quite incensed. He wrote to the insurance companies himself, but using his father's name, accusing them of defrauding his widow. Needless to say the 'widow' did not collect any money from the insurance policies, and as yet the insured man has not resurrected himself or returned to the UK.

Bank frauds

There is little doubt that there are frauds committed within banks, because wherever there is money there will be fraud, but outside fraud on banks also happens from time to time. A typical example is crossfiring of cheques — taking advantage of clearing delays to draw against 'uncleared effects' created for the purpose. In its simplest form it requires two bank accounts, both controlled by the fraudster. He pays into the first of these a cheque drawn on the second bank and, three days later when presentation of this cheque is effected through the clearing system, he meets it by paying into the second bank a cheque drawn on the first bank. The operation is repeated ad infinitum in both directions. Completely fictitious credit balances have thereby been created which could probably be drawn out in cash. If the amount of the cheque is constantly increased, the credit balances also increase. By the fraudster opening a third bank account the volume of the operation can be doubled, and a fourth bank account will treble it, and so on.

An example would be where the fraudster begins with three bank accounts and no money. He draws two cheques on each bank account and pays them into the other two bank accounts, starting at £100 and going up by £50 steps. In so doing he immediately creates balances of uncleared effects aggregating £1,350. On the second business day of the fraud he repeats the drawing and paying in operation, and his total balances now stand at £4,500. On the third business day he repeats the operation, paying in cheques for a total of £4,950 which therefore exceeds the first day's cheques of £1,350 which are now presented and have to be met. His balances, however, still increase by £3,600 to £8,100.

After nine business days, which is less than two weeks, his balances total a mere £29,700 so he decides to speed up the operation. To do this he draws £2,000 in cash on each of his three accounts and uses the £6,000 to open two more bank accounts with £3,000 each. He will now be drawing twenty cheques a day instead of six, but the step-up is reduced to £25. Three days later his balances have topped £150,000 on the twelfth business day of the operation. If the first business day of the operation was a Monday, the twentieth day will be a Friday four short weeks later, when the swindler draws £308,000 and still leaves £500 in each account to keep it warm over the weekend, while he disappears to warmer climes. On Monday and Tuesday the cheques lodged on the previous Thursday and Friday come home to roost and five bank managers are very unhappy.

Industrial espionage

Industrial espionage may not be fraud in the accepted sense of the word. It may not, in some cases, even be illegal but it is most certainly considered unethical. The loss of confidential information (trade secrets) can, just as with fraud, result in a financial loss to the company originating the information. Industrial espionage in effect is the stealing of secret or classified information and has been described as the seeking, obtaining and transmitting through secret means or false pretences, of industrial or commercial information for industrial, commercial, political or subversive purposes. Any business may be prone to industrial espionage if it has competitors who might be interested in its forward plans, its methods of business, new products, or any other attractive, useful material. The majority of businesses feel that it is unlikely they will be victims of industrial espionage, and they may be living with a sense of false security, for every company is prone to the threat.

All that is needed is one unscrupulous rival and most companies have these. Take for instance the firm of undertakers which found that its telephones were bugged and advised the police. It was found on investigtion that a rival firm of undertakers had hired a private investigator to install the bug. This was only part of the chain, for a whole network of links was established with hospitals, mortuaries and undertakers' parlours. The intelligence sought was the names and addresses of the bereaved, for undertaking is a business which is never in decline and involves a great deal of money. A macabre situation, but one which shows this kind of espionage can happen anywhere.

The Watergate Scandal proved that industrial espionage exists even at the highest level, but like computer fraud it is difficult to quantify. There are many factors which cause this situation.

(i)   A good spy is never discovered. Quite often a company which is the victim of industrial espionage is never aware of it.

(ii) When a leakage of information is discovered, this also becomes a secret, often more guarded than the stolen secrets. This is because an infiltrated company does not inspire much confidence. A public company might suffer a decline in its share price.

(iii) Very few discovered cases are reported for outside investigation because of fear of publicity.

Three types

Industrial espionage may be committed by any of three types of individual. An example of the first type is the opportunist who by accident finds himself in a position where he has access to a secret, or the trusted individual who realises the potential value of the information within his reach. Either of these may need money badly and will attempt to capitalise on the secret information to which they now have access. This sort of person has difficulty in knowing what to do with the stolen secrets. He can hardly put an advertisement in the press offering the secrets for sale. He may contact some of his employer's main competitors but this is hazardous, because the majority of companies, when offered such information, tell the victim or the police. Not all companies are so honest, though, and there are those who will be only too quick to cash in on the situation.

The second type of person likely to become involved in industrial espionage is the semi-professional, dubious private investigator. He is prepared to accept assignments, and is often hired to obtain a specific piece of knowledge. Because of his amateurish methods he stands a very good chance of discovery. One such example was a private detective who was hired by one of his colleagues in Europe to steal details of a process used by a company in Britain. If the plan was successful, details of this process were then to be sold to a European competitor.

The detective, as is the case with most amateurs, did not do the job himself but hired a young student to obtain details of the process, using her own initiative as to how she would do it. She had obviously read some spy books because she hired a taxi to drive her to the works where she took photographs. She then tried, without success to make contact with any useful person in the company. Eventually she decided to enlist the aid of the taxi driver. He was asked if he knew anyone in the company who would answer some questions about processes. He said that he did and offered to arrange a meeting between his alleged contact and the student. He reported the matter to the works manager and the meeting she sought was arranged, but not for the purpose she envisaged. The works manager carried recording equipment to the meeting where the student offered an initial payment of £150 for the information she required. She also hinted at more physical favours. Both the amateur detective and the student were prosecuted and convicted.

This sorry tale of amateurism is a long way from the more dangerous professional industrial espionage agent who devotes his life to, and gets his rewards from stealing and selling other people's secrets. It is believed that he does exist, and his whereabouts, like the contract killer, are known only to a few. Such a person may on the surface be very respectable and because of his expert knowledge may also be overtly engaged in countering industrial espionage. He is usually the sort of person who can approach a managing director and ask if he is interested in the processes of a competitor. Although this may bring rebuff, there are also acceptances.

The professional will not send a student to take photographs, but will himself research the company. He will ascertain the names of executive staff likely to have the information he is seeking. Having decided on his victim he will approach that person, possibly posing as a journalist for a well-known magazine. He will probably prefer to say he is from an overseas magazine, making the checking of his credentials more difficult, and say he is researching a story centred on the information he wishes to obtain. A clever professional will work on the vanity of his contact who will often be surprisingly frank with his answers. He will also, where necessary, use an associate to infiltrate the company as an employee to glean information.

The majority of information obtained by an industrial spy is through carelessness of management and staff. An infiltrator will search waste paper bins, change and take away executive typewriter ribbons and look at or photograph as many documents as possible. Even the most secure organisations can be infiltrated by a clever and determined person. It is unlikely that a confident person who appears to fit into the environment will be challenged. If he is, he usually has a good explanation. The successful industrial spy, like the successful fraudster, is always the first in and the last to leave. He is always the most knowledgeable and helpful and rarely takes holidays.

5   Electronic fraud

Computer technology has made a considerable impact upon our lives and our dependence on such technology can only be increased. Computer technology becomes more sophisticated daily and there is often a wide rift of knowledge between the executive/ manager and the computer specialist. The increase in computer specialisation merely widens that rift. This wide rift of knowledge can cause a lack of effective management which facilitates abuse of the system and allows interference to take place, at times totally unchecked.

A senior bank official who lectured at the Police College on fraud said:

> Having dwelt at some length on the position as it exists at present, the next question must be to forecast the effect on future frauds of a general introduction of computers. There is a widely held opinion that computers will make frauds virtually impossible. This I view with a considerable degree of scepticism.

His scepticism seems to have been justified.

Book-keeping methods have been in a state of flux throughout the last 50 years when accounting machines first made their appearance and they may have been undergoing constant changes even before that. As a result of these changes, methods of fraud have also had to change but frauds themselves have never ceased to flourish. In a manual system where additions had to be made without mechanical aid, all casts were re-checked as soon as there was a difference in the work, which was a daily occurence. This would have made some book-keeping frauds virtually impossible as they depend for success on the totals produced by machines being trusted implicitly. The introduction and the anonymity of accounting machines saved the culprit from having to make any fraudulent entries in his own handwriting which might have been recognised. Where the fraud is concerned with vouchers, whether with a manual system, a mechanical system or computers, the book-keeping still consists of vouchers and if these are dishonestly prepared or not prepared at all when they should be, the recording system will do no more than reflect them.

Business systems

Computers are playing an ever-increasing role in business systems. Management needs to know more about the operation and use of the system and also to ensure that internal auditors are effective in this environment. Internal auditors need to know how the computer works, what controls are required to safeguard against error and fraud, and how to use the computer for audit tests.

Computer fraud is probably the most talked about type of fraud. There are more seminars on the subject than virtually any other form of crime. This is probably because of the belief in companies' vulnerability in this area, and the fact that computers are used for almost every aspect of business. So what is computer fraud? One of the most difficult aspects of the subject is its true definition and many attempts have been made at it. One view is that a fraud should be regarded as a computer fraud if it could have occurred only because of the involvement of a computer. In other words, it is an unlawful act committed in a computer environment which depends in any way upon the attributes of the computer environment. Put more simply, it is fraudulent behaviour connected with computerisation by which someone intends to gain dishonest advantage. It has also been said that a computer fraud exists when there is an act of fraud causing an impact on the financial statement with a computer involved in the scheme. The last word should belong to the American computer manager who described it as equal opportunity employment with the job availability being bountiful as most computer training schools offer placement services included in the tuition fee. He went on to say: 'If the computer crook, however, cannot afford any business training he need not despair because he can enjoy a vocational course on computers as part of the rehabilitation programme in one of our penal institutions.'

Whichever way computer fraud is defined there is little doubt that it exists and that it is here to stay. Like all other crimes fraud will bring itself up to date and into the computer age. In 1986 a London branch of a major bank was believed to have lost over £440,000 to hackers. Although it has been suggested that none of the four big banks has escaped the attentions of the electronic fraudsters, reports from the other three show that one has not instigated any computer fraud prosecutions; one was 'unaware of any problems'; and the third refused to comment on whether or not there had been any prosecutions. But computer-related crime is now probably the world's biggest fraud growth industry, and in spite of what the banks have said, there are those who believe that tens of millions of pounds are being stolen through fraud annually in Britain alone. This belief would appear to be based on the awesome power of these electronic brains, and the fact that nearly a quarter of the free world's foreign exchange dealings now flow through the City of London.

A computer has no morals, no judgment and no common sense. It has been suggested that we are handing too much power to computers too soon. Even a computer's memory is not boundless and its contents have to be printed out periodically. If the print-outs are destroyed after the memory has been cleared, there is nothing left: not even all the little books and private records which flourished under the accounting machine systems. If programmers are not fraud-conscious they may not realise where they leave loop-holes for fraud.

Systems are often difficult to understand for staff other than computer staff. If someone does succeed in tampering with them, the chances of detection are often minimal. The extraordinary efficiency of a computer means that very little of its output is subjected to additional checks. Corrupt output will enjoy the same prestige as correct output. Even if a fraud is detected the culprit will often be shielded by the anonymity of the computer.

One thing which separates computer fraud from other types of fraud is the impersonal nature of the computer. A hacker can sit in front of a VDU and, depending on the security of the system, can have as many tries as he likes to gain access to the system. If he is successful the machine is at his mercy. If he has no luck then nothing is lost and there is no embarrassed confrontation with a supervisor. The word 'hacker' conjures up the image of an outsider infiltrating the most secret areas of business. This is perpetuated by film and television which dramatise stories of fraudsters, even children, who gain access to the most secure computer networks.

Hacking

In the context of computer crime hacking is the unauthorised entry into a computer system. It is the process whereby an individual, once having gained access to the system, looks around, leaves messages, runs programs, deletes or modifies programs or words, obtains information, or defrauds the system. Hackers can be divided into four main groups: (i) the experts; (ii) the swappers; (iii) the electronic vandals; and (iv) the criminals. Like many words in computing, hacker is a corruption of the true meaning of the word which was simply to be overworked or to work hard at something. In the earlier days of computers anyone working intensively with computers was a hacker. It was perhaps because of the concentration and long hours of work that the word, imported like most other computer words, from America, has now become an established part of the computer vocabulary. The most spectacular, and most difficult to commit, form of hacking is 'beating the system'. It is believed by some people to be the only true form of hacking. True hackers are like mountaineers: they break into computers because they are there and do it only for sport.

The criminal hacker can be a small-time criminal, or even an unintentional criminal, like the lovelorn young student who sent a girl flowers by breaking into a computer network. He used his home computer to break into the Prestel system, which allows users to order flowers and theatre tickets by linking their machines to the telephone. When caught, the young man said: 'I did it for a bit of fun—it was easy. I didn't even know I was breaking the law.' He also said that he did not know the girl had received the flowers until the police came round a year later. When asked about his hacking future he said: 'I haven't done any more hacking. Anyway they've confiscated my computer.'

The hacker can also be a person who is seeking information for gain. One such person was the hacker who, in 1984, broke into HRH Prince Philip's Prestel 'mail box'. This was a computer memory bank where messages could be left for him. But the hacker can also be a big-time criminal intent on making a fortune, such as the one who may have committed the crime alleged to have caused the loss of £440,000 to a major bank. Hacking, or electronic breaking and entering, need not be expensive for the hacker because it can be done with a home computer, a television set or monitor screen, software and a modem, together with a telephone link to the outside world. A modem can both dial out and answer calls, and an autodial modem can, in theory, persist with engaged numbers or work through a telephone book testing each number individually. This little box of tricks opens up the world for the hacker.

Passwords

It is now established that carelessness when selecting what to use as a password, and the lack of security of passwords, is the door-opener for most hackers. The hacker will try telephone numbers, birthdays, star signs, names of relatives or any other type of information which he gets to know about the victim, because it is from these areas of the victim's life that the password will probably be selected.

If users think that they cannot remember their passwords they will write them down. They will often make several copies to leave in handy places, such as taped to the terminal, in a nearby drawer, or pinned to the wall — an easy target for a good hacker. The computer itself can assist because it is good at boring repetitive tasks, like trying one password after another. Almost all hacking results from human error, and the fact that the computer cannot distinguish one operator from another except by the use of passwords which tell the computer to give access, and which are vulnerable to a determined hacker.

Who commits computer fraud, other than the hacker? Male computer fraudsters appear to outnumber female culprits by the ratio of four to one, although this is probably the same for other types of fraud. Male fraudsters seem to go for bigger stakes and richer pickings than the females. More outsiders and junior employees commit computer fraud than those holding managerial or supervisory positions. The more senior the fraudster, however, the greedier his scheme, and the higher the value of his fraud. Additionally, there is a percentage of cases which involves collusion between management and staff, in some cases with help from outsiders. The majority of frauds, however, are committed by computer users working in accounting, sales, invoicing, purchase or payroll departments.

Computer fraudsters are usually people who have unsupervised access to functions. They often have access to the entire system, or have a detailed knowledge of the system workings. They may be people who work a great deal of overtime or take few holidays. Computer fraud can take place only if the thief has access to the system, so by limiting the amount of access available to authorised users and preventing unauthorised access, the risks of fraud can be greatly reduced. (Computers that have communication links via the public telephone network are very vulnerable; a fraudster does not need to gain access to the premises, but does need specialist equipment.) The most common unauthorised access to computers is by using passwords intended to prevent or limit access to the application because they are inherently insecure. Popular passwords, those displayed for easy reference alongside terminals, or written on desk pads make it all too simple for the potential computer fraudster. Passwords should be regularly reviewed and changed to ensure that personnel are not gaining access to the system outside their authority.

It is axiomatic that fraud is more likely in poorly controlled and inefficient systems than in well run, clean and efficient ones. Frauds in poorly controlled systems are also less difficult to conceal and perpetuate. When the management of a company cannot rely on its computer output, even the most blatant symptoms of fraud can be overlooked as yet another error.

There is a wide variety of threats to the integrity of computer systems. Some are more likely to be exercised by certain personnel than by others, and in many cases the organisation seems to discard even routine checks and controls. Where no one would think of trusting an individual to develop and operate a manual system on their own, it is quite acceptable if they are using a computer. Users, especially clerical staff, will often exploit operational quirks of a system. It is users who tend to enter illegal transactions such as false orders and invoices, and they may collude to ignore checking procedures, or to deceive auditors. Computer operators are able physically to damage equipment in the computer room. They can reprint cheques or reports, and might substitute tapes or discs either in the installation, or while acting as couriers. They may also view and copy print-out reports.

Security tables are at risk from system programmers whose responsibility it is to maintain them. System programmers often have an in-depth knowledge of the computer which gives them a head start if they are contemplating computer fraud. The application programmers are those likely to use a 'Trojan Horse', which is a piece of fraudulent instruction in a utility program (*see* page 101). Systems analysts, on the other hand, because they may have designed or be responsible for the systems, are in a unique position to exploit quirks in the system. For instance, they can deliberately include hidden facilities when developing a system, and may also dictate access rights. One of the biggest areas of concern, however, is the expansion of personal computing because users who both develop and operate their own systems are in effect users, operators, systems and application programmers, and systems analysts all in one. Once the fraudster has gained access, there are a number of methods of manipulation that he can employ. These manipulations may be performed by anyone who has access to a terminal and a knowledge of how the applications are run.

Falsification or suppression of input

Input is of two basic kinds—transaction data and transaction entry codes. The falsification of input is positive when additional data is inserted, such as the inflation of purchase invoice values or the inflation of sales credits. It is negative when information such as sales data or purchase returns are suppressed prior to computer processing. Input can be corrupted, deliberately, so that the computer is unable to process it and rejects it into a suspense account or error cycle from which it can be manually manipulated.

When a falsification, positive or negative, takes place in the user department, the fraud is built into the control totals. Input and output balances should automatically agree. It is usually accepted in computing that if control totals or proof listing appear to be in agreement then the individual accounts and calculations supporting the totals must be correct. This is a very dangerous assumption: it is quite possible for control totals to be out of agreement with their subsidiary ledgers and accounts. Trade debtors' balances may not be supported by the subsidiary personal accounts of customers, or crossfiring may have occurred in individual accounts, without affecting control totals.

Passive injection

Paaive injection is the use of a system's ordinary facilities to enter undetected, but illegal, information. It exploits the fact that the system does not adequately validate all transactions. Transactions are direct operations, such as the entry of an invoice, the registering of a customer or the recording of an order. The fraudster may operate one of two methods:

(i)   he may enter any illegal transactions through the usual methods; or

(ii)   he may transmit his own data via a communications line or network.

Manipulation of master files

The manipulation of master files may be positive or negative. False entries of value per unit sales or purchases, credit limits, discount rates, price zones, and others can be placed on to a master file so that when the transaction data is processed it results in a false credit to a personal account, and a consequential debit concealed in a loosely controlled account. These frauds are easy to manipulate and do not leave an audit trail once the fraud has been committed. A master file might be amended only momentarily while a transaction is being fraudulently processed. After processing, the correct price or information can be replaced in the master file.

Manipulation of suspense accounts

In most systems, in whatever mode they run, there will be some transactions which, for one reason or another, will be rejected into an error cycle, pipeline or suspense account. These are vulnerable to fraud since they are often left to one person to resolve and can be concealed outside the normal transaction balancing.

Misuse of restricted utilities

Restricted utilities are pieces of software that are available on any computer system. They enable the user to gain direct access to and alter computer disk memory. They may be used to change, add or delete items directly, without any evidence of their use showing on control reports. The misuse of these utilities is also known as 'superzap' (*see* page 100).

Program patching

Programs which process data can be rigged with 'patches', or may be overlaid by adding extra instructions. This will divert transaction data which may cause the program to handle some or all of the information it is processing in a fraudulent manner. The patch may be in an application program, in the operating sytem or in job control statements. Such frauds are not easy to commit and are even more difficult to detect.

Job control manipulation

Job controls direct the process of a computer application; they tell the computer which programs to run and what files to use. By changing job controls a programmer can re-direct the applications and use programs and/or files that have been tampered with.

Hardware modification

Computer hardware may be rigged to give incorrect results. Normally the skills and knowledge required to carry out even the simplest of these manipulations are limited to systems support personnel. They will usually enjoy free access to the computer equipment, but will have very limited opportunity to convert any fraudulent manipulation into goods or cash. It is possible, however, that the same skills and knowledge could be acquired by other personnel with free access to the computer equipment, although this would take time and extensive use of facilities.

Worldwide problem

The fear of computer fraud is worldwide; most countries are aware of the problem and are taking steps to deal with it. The United States has experienced more than most in terms of computer-related crime. There the problem has been analysed in greater depth than elsewhere and investigators have been trained more extensively to investigate it. Most of what is written about computer related-crime originates in the United States.

That computer-related fraud assumes a greater importance in the United States is probably because American law on the subject is more clearly defined than in most other countries. By law, all financial institutions which have suffered from computer abuse, not just financial fraud, must report their losses to the federal authorities. The Federal Bureau of Investigation has probably the most expert personnel in the world trained in computer fraud investigation.

One of America's best-known computer fraud cases was that of Stanley Mark Rifkin. He used a wire fraud to transfer 10.2 million dollars from the Security Pacific National Bank, through an account at the Irving Trust Company of New York and a Russian diamond dealer in Geneva. Rifkin was able to walk into the wire transfer room at Security Pacific and look at a notice on the wall which listed the 'secret' code numbers which he used in test keys. Security Pacific were told by the FBI of what had happened and it was only then that they discovered they were missing the 10.2 million dollars. Rifkin did not get away with it: he blew the whole operation by smuggling diamonds into the United States, bought with his illicit gains, and tried to unload some of them in California.

Japan has reported fraudulent extraction of money in a multiplicity of ingenious ways. Theft from automatic cash dispensers is currently the greater problem there. Computer-related fraud as we think of it is not yet regarded as a serious issue and it is only now that more attention is being focused on this growing problem.

Hong Kong is facing an increasing amount of computer-related crime and both managers and investigators lack the computer skills to deal with the problem.

West Germany closely follows the United States in its attitudes to computer fraud, whereas the Swiss, even though Zurich and Geneva are world centres of finance with highly automated systems, do not seem to have a problem with computer-related fraud on the scale one might imagine.

Canada, also follows similar patterns of computer abuse to those of the United States, although the number of incidents is substantially less. Sweden undertook a comprehensive survey of computer-related crime: it acknowledged the difficulty of defining what constitutes computer-related crime and found it hard to make an accurate estimate. Australia, on the other hand, appears to be facing a considerable problem in the field of computer-related crime and was one of the first to produce a computer abuse case book.

In Britain there have, over the last few years, been several attempts to determine the level of computer fraud, but without central recording this is a very difficult task. The police, when looking at the question of whether or not to set up a training course in the investigation of computer-related crime, did a survey of such crimes reported to the police on a force basis. This was done in the early 1980s and revealed that only 21 cases of computer-related crime had been reported to the police in the whole of the United Kingdom; all of them were fairly simple and straightforward matters to investigate. From the point of view of the police the situation is not dissimilar today.

The Local Government Audit Inspectorate surveyed computer fraud in both 1981 and 1985 with slightly differing results, although the different criteria for inviting participation in the two surveys is thought to be a main reason for the variations in the two results. The 1981 survey produced 319 replies of which 79 per cent said that they had suffered a computer fraud in the last five years. They reported 67 cases of computer fraud, varying from £250 to £250,000, yielding for the fraudsters £905,149.

The 1985 survey produced 943 replies of which 92 per cent said that they had suffered a computer fraud in the last five years. They reported 77 cases, again varying from £250 to £250,000, and yielding £1,133,487 for the fraudsters.

There have been other surveys, and one taken at a seminar revealed that of a total of 42 persons surveyed only one considered computer fraud to be a major problem at the present time, although 26 considered that it would be a major problem in the future.

Jargon of fraud

Computer fraud has its own jargon and different types of computer fraud are given descriptive names. Some examples are given below.

Salami fraud

A fraud which involves manipulating a large number of small amounts of money. Called 'salami' because the fraud occurs in small slices. An example of a salami fraud is one which occurred in the United States: a few extra lines of coding were introduced in a bank interest calculation program, to credit small rounding-down differences on all customers' accounts to the fraudulent programmers' account.

Scavenging

If the computer's main memory is not zeroised after a program has been run, some details of the computer file which the program used are retained in the computer's main memory. It is technically just possible that another user with access to the computer could read these remnants of perhaps very confidential information. It is very unlikely, however, that there would be enough information to be of value, and in this form the data would be incomprehensible anyway. Scavenging can also mean checking through the refuse from computer installations looking for print-outs which have been discarded, but which may contain confidential information.

Superzap

This is the name of an IBM program which can be used to change pieces of data in files or programs. Superzap circumvents the normal security precautions. It is usually used to solve one-off problems in computer installations. A systems programmer who has access to superzap could, for example, change his, or anyone else's, salary in the files. Most computer manufacturers offer products with similar facilities.

Logic bomb and time bomb

A logic bomb is a manipulation of a program which conducts a series of events triggered by logical sequence. Many computers offer the facility to delay the execution of a program until a specified date and time. They automatically run the program at regular intervals each hour, day, week, month or year. It is often essential automatically to take back-up copies of important data files in case the computer develops a fault, or to log the usage of the terminals, or to close down certain facilities. Abused, this can allow someone to create programs which seriously corrupt or destroy data files at some time in the future, or over a period of time. A time-bomb is an unauthorised code in the program which conducts a series of events triggered by a specific date and time. All mainframe computers have an internal clock. This allows programs to check the current time and date against a date which has been coded into the program. One classification of time bombs, therefore, is a destructive piece of coding in a program which will take effect only after a specific date. Another variation of a time bomb is coding which will only take effect after a pre-determined event has occurred. For example, a programmer, who was on bad terms with his management, inserted a time bomb into one of his company's salary programs. The destructive coding caused the salaries file, and a number of other essential files, to be overwritten by rubbish when the programmer's own record was deleted from the salaries file if and when he was dismissed.

Trojan Horse

Programs have every right to be in the computer—they are the lists of instructions that make the machine work. In security terms they represent 'Trojan Horses'—objects which are outwardly like any other, but which carry a deadly surprise. In other words, a Trojan Horse is a piece of fraudulent instruction in a utility program. This is a program which carries out certain routine aspects of processing, and is likely to be used by many application programs in the installation. The fraudulent programming of the utility program is therefore surreptitiously introduced into the applications program. A Trojan Horse was used to transfer high privilege authority to access any files from a legitimate program to a fraudulent programmer's program.

Data diddling

This fraud is one in which data is changed before, or whilst it is being fed into the computer.

Piggy backing

This occurs when an unauthorised person fraudulently impersonates a user with authority to gain access to the computer system.

Trap doors

These are computer program instructions which allow an unauthorised user fraudulently to sidestep requirements by taking advantage of weaknesses in the design, logic or electronic circuitry of the system.

Disgruntled employees

The most worrying of these computer frauds are the ones committed by disgruntled employees with high levels of technical knowledge who sabotage the company's computer programs by planting their time or logic bombs to go off months after the employee has disappeared from the records. They may even destroy any data that the employer attempts to re-enter from back-up storage.

It is believed that at least 15 crimes of this nature have recently been identified. The sabotage has in some cases been so extreme that the victim company has been 'bombed' into liquidation. One such crime, although not so extreme as to cause liquidation, was committed by an employee who was dismissed and took with him the full list of trade outlets which he attempted to sell to a competitor. He had left a time bomb in the system which was intended to destroy the system if he was detected in his activities. He was discovered, whereupon he warned his former employers about the time bomb, without giving any details, so that they were forced to bring in an expert to trace it. The expert made a search, but unfortunately he triggered the time bomb. This was a serious blow to the company and one which could potentially have caused very serious disruption to their business and loss of a great deal of sales. They were, however, lucky because when offering the stolen information to a competitor the dismissed employee had allowed them to retain the information for examination. They had secretly made a copy of the information and returned it to the company from which it had been stolen.

Computers have brought with them a new language, and a new breed of criminal competent to commit highly technical frauds. The fraudsters have learned how to adapt to the computer age, and are aware that computers make fraud more difficult to recognise and investigate. Organised crime may seize the opportunity to use computer technology to its advantage but, so far, the majority of computer crimes dealt with in Britain are committed by individuals and generally, as with other frauds, they are those with previously good characters.

The growing awareness of computer-related crime poses a difficult problem for both management and investigator, and in both cases they must become familiar with computers and computer language. It is not, however, all on the side of the criminal, because not all computer-literate people are criminals. Many people with computer training and knowledge are becoming managers, directors and investigators. It is a matter of matching their skills with those of the fraudster, and of being aware of the problem.

6 Prevention and detection

Three elements

The only sure way to prevent fraud is to be aware that it exists, that it can happen to you and to take positive action to minimise the risk. Like all other crime, fraud will always exist as long as there is money or there are goods to steal and there are people in a position and of a mind to steal them. No system is totally secure, whether it is computerised or not, and the longer a system has been in operation the more likely it is that it can be breached by fraud.

By definition, perfect crime, computer-related or not, escapes detection and high-level, technologically brilliant schemes are made possible. Even so, the greatest losses to fraud arise through simple and obvious gaps in a system of control. The easier the opportunity for fraud, the more likely it is to be exploited. It is also likely to be exploited more often by more people. All frauds have three elements, all of which are identifiable, and only one of them needs to be discovered for the whole of the fraud to be revealed. The three elements are set out below.

The act of theft

This is committed by the physical transfer of an asset or a business interest to the thief. Even in the most complex computer fraud this act will be outside computing processes and will be detectable and provable by normal investigative methods.

The act of concealment

This is committed by the falsification of the accounts to conceal the theft or to prepare the way for the act of theft without further concealment. This will similarly be outside computing.

The act of conversion

The item stolen needs to be converted or manipulated in the accounts into a value suitable to the thief. Proper controls exercised by the victim will usually limit the computer's use in fraud to things such as the creation of false accounting credit in balance books, and the suppression of the consequential debit in a loosely controlled account.

In the early days of a fraud criminals are more likely to make mistakes, since they rarely hit on a method which suits them right away. All losses and all errors should, where possible, be investigated at once in order to minimise the opportunity for fraud. In any case there should be a strictly controlled check system in respect of losses and errors.

If fraud detection is to act as a deterrent it is not necessary to detect all frauds. It is necessary, however, that some frauds are detected so that persons contemplating fraudulent or dishonest acts are uncertain that they will succeed without getting caught. Further, it is not necessary for a thief to be detected in his most brilliant fraud, as any detection which is sufficient to prove his guilt will be adequate to prosecute and dismiss him. The threat of detection does not scare an honest man, but people fear things they do not understand. A dishonest programmer may be aware of the controls within computing but may fear controls in other areas of the business with which he is not familiar. He should be made to fear the efficiency of managers, even those with whom he does not come into contact. Basic controls need to be enforced if they are to work and should always be looked at from the position of a person comtemplating crime. Company-wide defences are therefore the best means of controlling fraud.

Risk of fraud

If a company has dishonest employees then there is a greater risk of fraud being committed. A prime method of prevention is to try to ensure that previously dishonest people are not employed unless they are prepared to disclose their crimes. When selecting personnel, it may help to ask the question: 'Why did you leave your previous employment?' Application forms for jobs should include a question about a person's possible criminal record. In most circumstances the police are not allowed, by law, to divulge a person's criminal record for the purposes of employment, but this would not preclude a question on the application form such as: 'Would you be prepared to allow us to check with the police as to whether or not you have a criminal record?' If the candidate for the job has a criminal record and has no intention of telling you about it, he will probably not proceed beyond this stage and will throw the form away rather than answer the question.

It is essential that all questions are answered and the applicant challenged if vague replies are given. References must be taken up, not only to protect the company, but also probably to comply with the requirements of insurers who underwrite fidelity cover. Testimonials should, where possible, be checked to ensure that they are genuine, or that there is not something which the writer would prefer to tell you on enquiry. Any testimonial which does not clearly indicate its sources should be treated with great suspicion, and be the subject of very searching questions. If the testimonial does give its source, further enquiries should be made of the person who wrote it, to establish if there are any conflicting interests. If a person claims to have a degree or other qualification, especially if one of the qualifications for employment is the holding of such a degree or qualification, the facts should be checked. Do not be satisfied with the word of the prospective employee: make proper checks to ensure that he is telling the truth. Some people, especially those who have a criminal bent, will ignore the fact that a degree or qualification is required and will apply for the post anyway. Sometimes they will give vague references which will lead to the belief that they hold such a degree or qualification, but equally they may untruthfully claim to have the degree or qualification with nothing to back up that claim, but in the hope that they will not be asked for proof.

Case in point

A company who required an engineer to take charge of a major section of a multi-million pound contract in a foreign country interviewed a man who, in his initial application, indicated that he held the required qualifications. At the interview these qualifications, were not discussed, much to the company's eventual regret. He did not hold any of the qualifications which he had put on his application form, but he was a superb con man with previous convictions for fraud, who was not going to let simple things like qualifications spoil his chances. He had changed his name by deed poll to one which sounded very upper class and had done a lot of preparation for the interview so that he was able to trot out impressive technical jargon.

Not one of the candidate's claims was checked and he was appointed to a very important post purely on an interview in which he had charmed the interviewers, who felt it 'not proper' to ask such a well-qualified man too many questions. The results were soon to show. He was sent abroad to take over the contract and was given responsibility for a very large budget with access to bank accounts. He spent very little of the money on the project but ran up enormous debts with sub-contractors, both for work done and for personal loans for which he gave company IOUs. He also drew large sums of money from the bank accounts, in cash, and was quite unable to account for it. He was such a dyed-in-the-wool con man that when he took a prostitute as a girlfriend he did not pay her on a regular basis. Instead he gave her a high-value, post-dated, company cheque, and allowed her to buy items of jewellery on his company credit cards.

Eventually things began to show and he was summoned back to England to answer questions. He was not dismissed, however, because although he took advantage of the fact that the company paid his airfare home, he did not turn up at his final interview but disappeared. The company was left with enormous debts from his activities, and their customers lost confidence in them. Simple checks to verify his qualifications could well have saved all this from happening.

Staff duties

Another effective means of preventing fraud is by segregation of staff duties. Often this is not done because of economic reasons or because of a limited number of staff. It is essential if the risk of fraud is to be eliminated, or reduced, that staff duties should be periodically reorganised even if careful planning is necessary. No one person should be responsible for the whole of a transaction and the scope of a person's duties must be clearly defined and limits of responsibility established. Members of staff should never be allowed to exceed the defined limits and if this happens then the reasons should be ascertained and checked. It is essential that cross checks are built into the system so that work performed by any employee is automatically checked by another. It is not sufficient, however, simply to build in these checks and hope that they work. The checking system must also be scrutinised occasionally to ensure that it is being carried out. It is not unknown for a checker simply to take the word of a fraudster that his work is accurate and pass it through. The greatest risk is when an employee has access to both accounting records and assets.

Somewhere in an organisation there may be an employee who drives to the office in his new, top-of-the-line Jaguar car from his large home with extensive grounds and stables. At work, he is responsible for all bankings, looks after the payroll and does bank reconciliation. He may also send out statements, prepare and pay disbursement cheques and have access to the sales and purchases ledgers. If there is such an employee the company may just have a problem. Such people will usually disobey instructions and then explain that it was not possible to comply. They may also spend a lot of time providing information on an 'I thought you ought to know' basis. This is often used to cover up their own activities, and to stop anybody asking questions in the belief that they have already been told.

No holidays

There are employees who will not take any holidays or, if they do, they will come into the office daily just to make sure that everything is alright. It may be that they are over conscientious, but they could be covering up fraudulent activities (see Supervisor Fraud, page 30). It is also vitally important that staff are sufficiently trained in other jobs to cover for holidays or other periods of absence. A fraudster will try to ensure that all his work is left whilst he is away and that no one else is able to check what he has been doing. He will exploit confusion. If someone is standing in for an absent employee it is essential that any queries which arise should, where possible, be resolved immediately and not left for the absent employee to deal with on his return. If the query cannot be resolved it should be given more than ordinary attention. Never hire a temporary employee to take over a sensitive position. It is surely better to have one of the typists from the pool trained for holidays, sickness and other absences, and to use the temporary employee in the pool.

As has already been stated, being aware that fraud does exist, and may well do so in any company, can go a long way towards preventing it. It is first necessary to establish the attitude of directors and managers towards fraud. If possible a meeting should be arranged at senior level to discuss the subject. This will increase the general awareness of the potential problems. If it is felt that a meeting devoted to fraud is unnecessary, it could be included as an item on the agenda for management meetings. Taking a close look at departmental structure can help to evaluate the risk, and this might be coupled with a review of all key controls to ensure that they are adequate. If these do not exist or are loosely controlled the door has been left wide open. If fraud is suspected it must be dealt with immediately. Too often, doing little or nothing provides the fraudster with the opportunity to take evasive action or to cover his tracks.

Files and documents

It is essential to safeguard files and valuable documents which might tempt a thief who will hope to make money out of information. It is usual to classify files as secret or confidential and to mark the files with their own classification, or to colour code them. Unfortunately, this makes it easy for the thief to identify the files which are worth looking at if they are left lying about. It is a natural human trait to want to look at something which is forbidden. If such files are kept, consideration might be given to a secure and central registry with a clear set of instructions for the handling and transmission of the files.

Security is also essential where premises, safes and alarms are concerned. It is amazing how many departments and offices are left unattended during the lunch break; and how many premises have been left insecure at night simply through lax security. It seems that some people choose to leave the alarm key on top of the control box, and the safe keys in an office drawer. An unattended office computer can easily be powered up, the database compromised, and the system powered down, all within minutes, and no one may ever find out that the damage was done. Some proprietary computer packaged systems offer little or no safeguards against unauthorised access to business data and software but a relaxed approach to security can be very costly. And it takes an awful lot of explaining to the insurance companies once the unthinkable has happened.

When staff leave

Consideration should be given to the measures adopted with staff who are about to leave. Good recruitment and termination procedures, along with regular progress reviews of staff performance, help to provide early warning of disgruntled employees. They help to initiate preventive measures, and to pre-empt possible abuse of the system.

Although termination interviews are usually a means of detection, rather than a prevention of fraud, they should be built into routine controls. It is surprising what can be learned about a company during this type of interview. Many employees do not give the true reason why they are leaving. A properly conducted termination interview might yield a lot of information as to what is going on. For the time it takes and the possible benefits it is a well worthwhile exercise. This can be particularly true where computer personnel are concerned. Employees leaving their companies have been caught removing sensitive corporate information and valuable programs. Always be conscious of time bombs. It is worth remembering when an employee in the computer department is leaving, particularly if the reason is unknown or he is to be dismissed, that he can cause havoc in a system if so minded. It might be expedient to exercise far more supervision during the last few days of such a person's employment, or even to transfer them to other duties. If such a person is dismissed from his employment then it is essential that he is escorted from the premises and not allowed to touch the computer, no matter for what excuse. The operation of just one key can cause havoc. Not only in the computer department but throughout the company, the risks should be considered. There is no point becoming paranoid about computer fraud if all other, maybe potentially more dangerous, losses are ignored.

General security

As far as the general security within the computer department is concerned, checks and prevention measures should be a regular part of the system. It is always worthwhile having a periodic check on the system, and the following are some of the questions which might be asked.

- How often are passwords changed?
- How strict are the checks on transactions users terminals?
- Are passwords given to individuals, or do they refer to anyone in a group?
- What measures are taken to prevent programmers:
  running their own illicit programs?
  illicitly amending existing ones during maintenance?
- What steps are taken to ensure that:
  all testing is done on separate test files?
  sensitive systems undergo program recompiling and comparison of the object code?
- What is done if the terminal system indicates a security violation?
- Can the editor be used to edit data files?
- What happens when:
  a user leaves a terminal for a prolonged period of time?
  payroll reports or cheques are printed?
- Is a member of the salaries or accounts section present in the computer room?
- How do you deal with computer staff who are leaving? Are all their access rights removed?
- Are all sensitive test/out-of-date reports shredded?
- Are all security staff on systems analyst's list of 'People to See' when developing a new system?
- What is done to prevent or trace those involved in inserting private fraud routines, such as the salami technique (*see* page 99), to round down transaction amounts and build up residues in special accounts?
- Could a Trojan Horse be introduced into your system? If so, what is being done to prevent or detect such an occurrence which may have been introduced to suppress printing of warning messages or to write off outstanding debts. Such schemes could prove extremely difficult to detect as the illegal code is activated only by very special switches, and may not come to light even with extensive testing. Good authorisation procedures for program amendments, followed by diligent

checking of changed coding from independent persons would help to minimise the success of Trojan Horse schemes.

- What controls are provided on remote terminals? Opportunities abound for culprits who are authorised terminal users to use the remote terminal for their own purposes. Such use might involve entering fraudulent transactions, retrieving information to plan for private gain, or even abusing the special facilities provided for terminal users, including the misuse of training facilities to defraud their employers. Checks should also be made on the security of items such as micro-computers or visual display units which may be portable.

Reducing risk

It is essential that risks which could result in high losses, or a catastrophic impact on business, should be avoided if the business is to remain viable. The cost of implementing direct countermeasures has to be balanced against probable levels of direct and consequential losses. Nevertheless, risk reduction methods should be examined in detail to reduce the possibility, or frequency, or severity of loss.

Reduction or prevention, detection and recovery measures can be implemented through the installation of protection equipment and software. They can also be implemented by the appointment of control and security personnel, by setting up control and reporting procedures, or by providing security training to improve general awareness of risks, and taking effective action to minimise losses.

Failure to appreciate the need for proper segregation of duties in key functions has resulted in many frauds being successful. Unfortunately, some small companies can ill afford the luxury of separate manning for input, data control, system design, programming and computer operation. This means that as more small business computers come into use in individual business departments, unless more attention is given to the control and auditability of business applications, more organisations will fall prey to clandestine activities by rogue staff. Suitable training on computer security is necessary to increase the security awareness of staff.

Regular reviews of job reruns and system access violation would help to pinpoint the various causes of errors and ommissions or potential abuse, and to determine appropriate corrective action to enhance operation performance and data integrity.

Fraud-detection computer models could be designed by the computer auditor to facilitate policing of the company's business activities. These would help abnormal activities to be spotted more quickly and enable action to be taken to curtail further damage to the company. Contingency planning plays a key role to ensure the continued survival of an organisation. A company which operates with a clear management style, has good personnel practices and uses effective control, is less likely to suffer from fraud. In a company that has weak or dishonest management and poor controls, fraud is not only possible, it is almost inevitable.

Detection

If fraud prevention does not work, the next step must be fraud detection. When the concept of delegating the catching of criminals to a police force was first conceived, the original members were put into a uniform so that they would be easily recognised. This was based on the assumption that it would help those in need to recognise quickly where to go to seek help. It was also seen as a crime prevention measure in that a person who was about to commit a crime would think again if a uniformed officer was in sight.

The result was that because of the presence of the uniformed officers some criminals did not in fact pursue their intention to commit a crime. But the vast majority of criminals simply waited until the uniform was out of sight, then got on with their criminal business. So came the birth of the detective, who wore plain clothes and was indistinguishable from other people. Even when detection is almost certain there will always be those who are willing to have a go.

There is no easy way of detecting fraud, which has usually involved careful planning and a lot of hard work. A study carried out for the *Computer Fraud & Security Bulletin* showed that frauds were detected or disclosed through the following sources:

Accident	51 per cent
Disgruntled mistresses	20 per cent
Auditors	19 per cent

Management controls   10 per cent

On this basis it could be argued that it would be most effective to pray that in this area you are accident prone; to fire the internal auditor; and to encourage key personnel to take a mistress then set about disgruntling them!

Most of the suggestions which have been given for fraud prevention will also serve to identify frauds which are in the process of being committed; but never overlook the obvious. It is well worth considering employees' life styles. You may discover that you have a junior employee whose second car, the one he does not drive to work, is a Porsche. He could possibly have paid for it with a legacy left by a great-aunt, but on the other hand he could just have his own 'business' using your facilities.

Look for deviations. Examination of marketing reports might highlight a variation in the purchasing pattern of a customer where there is no apparent reason for it. Follow it through and check it out. Give full attention to the weakest, most simple inconsistency when hunting out a suspected fraud. Look at the three elements — the act of theft, the act of concealment and the act of conversion — as one of these will have presented the greatest problem to the thief (*see* page 103). Identify which of the three will produce the most obvious symptoms of fraud then concentrate on that element. Do not dismiss your findings as impossible when you discover that the suspect is one who has always been regarded as a trusted employee. If, after an investigation of all the facts, the guilt appears to lie with one person, the chances are that he *is* the guilty party.

Stock losses, inflation of expenses and assets, suppression of sales and liabilities, deviation from normal practices or procedures, missing documents, and distortion of historical or proportional trends are all major symptoms of fraud. Once the initial symptoms have been identified and the fact that a fraud is being committed has been detected, the investigation still has to begin. This can be tedious and time consuming, but the effort is usually worthwhile, especially if some simple rules, which have general application to both fraud detection and investigation, are followed.

(1)   Never overlook the obvious.

(2)   Never seek the most complex solution to tracing a possible fraud.

(3)   Always concentrate first on the more simple elements of the fraud.

(4)   Never try to solve the whole problem at one go. If possible, break the fraud down into small easily provable parts which can be looked at separately.

(5)   If a fraud has been concealed, suspect the person who has access to a course of concealment and whose guilt, without concealment, would have been most obvious.

(6)   Assign your resources to the best advantage.

(7)   Do not worry if your first line of attack leads to nothing: try the next line.

(8)   Make fraud detection a routine part of your business. Do not treat it as a simple one-off exercise whenever fraud is suspected.

(9)   Remember that criminals become uncertain whenever there is a fear of detection, and that is when they make their more obvious mistakes.

(10)   If you believe that there is a series of frauds do not attempt to detect them all at once. Concentrate on the more simple and easily detectable: you may end up with a full confession.

(11)   If, after a preliminary investigation the evidence appears to point to a particular person, the chances are that he is responsible.

(12)   The easiest opportunities for fraud are the ones most likely to have been exploited.

(13)   It is not necessary to detect computer fraud in computing; there may be other more simple solutions.

(14)   Fraud detection is time-consuming, hard work, but these two elements will produce the result required.

(15)   Once the fraudster is caught, do not assume that he will wait around for you to complete your investigations.

(16)   It is unsafe to accept, without question, that control accounts agree with subsidiary ledgers.

(17)   The essence of successful fraud is that honest people should not suspect it is taking place.

(18)   When verifying purchases, always work from ledger accounts back to source records.

A test

It is always possible that before you suspect a person is committing fraud his conduct will indicate that he may be involved in bribery and corruption, particularly if he is a buyer or involved in the purchases department. If bribery and corruption are suspected a test should be carried out which may give a clear indication that corruption is taking place and fraud being committed. If the tests are positive then it is essential that a closer look is taken at that person's work, life style and contacts. In order to carry out this test, first of all select a small number of contracts handled by the purchasing or contracts department, and be particularly wary when the following circumstances apply:

- the supplier has no published price list;
- the contract is on a cost plus basis;
- the contractor's charges are supported by third party invoices;
- costs appear above normal for the industry;
- the goods supplied are outside the contractor's normal line of business;
- the goods supplied are for a section of a department not subjected to usual controls, or are experimental;
- the contractor is frequently awarded contracts without competition, or is frequently the lowest tenderer;
- the goods supplied by the contractor appear to be sub-standard;
- the contract involves over-runs;
- the contract is just below a central or board level authority limit;

- the contract is well below other tenders, and there is an amount set aside for contingency;
- little detail is shown on contract documents;
- pages are missing from a tender;
- supporting charges cannot be checked;
- there is a clause requiring discounts on goods supplied or used to be passed on, yet no discounts ever appear on invoices.

Check out other tenderers submitting competitive bids and look for connections, such as:
- the contractor is not listed in the telephone book or no telephone number is given;
- correspondence from several tenders has a common printing layout.

Physically examine work done, and if possible speak to some of the contractor's employees. Endeavour to examine the contractor's work records and accounts. If there is payment for labour, check that the persons, or the number of persons, alleged to be on site are physically there. Do not make this check at a regular time of day.

Computer fraud presents its own difficulties in detection and investigation, because computers have brought with them a new language. The crimes committed involve a different breed of criminal and are frequently committed by individuals with a previously good character.

The growing awareness of computer-related crime poses a difficult problem for investigators, and for management in training personnel to combat this growing menace. Not only is training required in detection and possible investigation, but every manager will need to be familiar with computers and computer jargon. One wrong move can leave you with the knowledge that a fraud has been committed but you are unable to do anything about it. The people to beware are often highly-regarded employees, who have access to an entire system, or have a knowledge of the entire systems workings. Such persons may work much overtime and take few holidays. If you discover any of these combinations and suspect fraud, or if you catch the culprit at it, then plan the trap very carefully because you must beware distributed processing, remote 'dial-in' access, and the possible destruction of evidence.

Having found the suspect, the next important step should be to isolate him rapidly from all access whilst you collect evidence. If the keys to your house are stolen it is prudent to change the locks. Similarly, if a suspect is suspended or sacked it is essential that access numbers to the system are changed immediately and that the suspect is not allowed free access to the computer room. It is as well in these circumstances to have an expert along, and these days police Fraud Squads have a growing expertise in computer fraud investigation. They can assist in collecting the program listings, run diagrams, job schedules, job accounting reports, terminal access logs, computer operations log and fault log. All of these will need to be examined depending on the type of fraud suspected. It is no use allowing the suspect to empty his own desk without supervision, and the same applies to his locker. His car and home may need to be searched for discarded print-outs, job execution sheets and other incriminating matters, and the police will be able to assist in this. The next step in the investigation will be to check the program listings for unauthorised amendments, but in most cases you will be looking for input documents. The ones you will require are those which have been altered in some way or are completely false.

The floppy disk can cause several problems because it can very easily be secreted about the person. It can also be damaged beyond recovery in a matter of seconds, so care in handling them is essential, and precautions need to be taken to preserve this type of evidence. The computer fraud investigations sections of police Fraud Squads are now well trained in this area. They have detailed systems, developed through years of experience, for searching business premises and detailing exhibits found. Computers and computerised documents make little difference, they have the knowledge and the expertise to handle them.

Like general fraud in its early days, when the police quite often wrote it off as unsatisfactory business, there is presently a lack of confidence by business management in the professional ability of the police to investigate these more technically-oriented frauds. There is also the problem that both the victim and the computer company feel somewhat embarrassed over a simple fraud against their system, and by the unlawful use of and access to their systems.

There is a further and more menacing reason why computer fraud may not be reported to the police. This is that companies often prefer to use an outside independent computer security consultant to investigate and tighten up their systems, and then ask the guilty party to resign. There is absolutely no reason why a professional independent security consultant should not be employed to assist in the detection of fraud and examination of the systems, but when a fraudster is caught he should be reported to the police for full investigation and prosecution. Any company that adopts the policy of simply sacking the culprit is asking for trouble. Other employees are quick to find out about this weakness and to abuse it. This has been found out time after time, very often at substantial cost. The best antidote to crime is tight controls, and if there is *still* fraud, the apprehension and conviction of the offender must follow.

The fight against fraud

In spite of the growth of investigative agencies the incidence of fraud in business has become much more common in the last ten years, especially in relation to purchasing. This was highlighted in the results Dr Michael Levi's survey, *see* page 15. The report of the survey said that although recorded fraud had increased considerably this century, the increase has recently become more pronounced. For example, since 1980 the crime of fraud has increased by 5 per cent per annum and, in 1984, £687 million was either actually or potentially lost through those frauds recorded by police Fraud Squads in London alone.

Around 40 per cent of large United Kingdom companies have been the victims of at least one fraud involving over £50,000 in the last ten years and the report estimates that commercial fraud is costing British firms about £1 billion a year. Furthermore, it is revealed that over 70 per cent of those committing fraud were employees of the company concerned, who occasionally worked with outsiders. In order to fight this growing menace there have been calls for a more rigorous policing of frauds in order to encourage companies to be more forthcoming in reporting them.

It seems that many companies see fit to conduct their own thorough enquiry before the police are called in. They do this, apparently, in order to present the police with a detailed scenario on which to take action because their confidence in the police to carry out an investigation is not very strong. It is essential that with the growing incidence of fraud, businessmen must be able to have complete confidence in the investigative agencies to carry out full and accurate investigations quickly and competently. In order to meet this need, police Fraud Squads have increased in size and number over the last few years, but it is a sad fact that at present only about 5 per cent of police manpower is allocated to the investigation of these crimes, with little or no career structure within the

119

fraud departments. In spite of this the police have sought to increase the expertise of their fraud investigators by introducing longer and more specialised fraud investigation courses. In order to combat the increasing incidence of computer fraud many police officers attended the FBI Academy in the United States to study computer fraud investigation techniques. Recently a specialist Computer Fraud Investigation Techniques Course was introduced at the Police College at Bramshill which can take many more students than could possibly be sent to America.

This course in now an established part of the Police College training scheme and students who have attended from all parts of the United Kingdom are competent to investigate computer fraud. These students, after completion of the course, also lecture to their colleagues who have not yet had the benefit of such training.

The office of the Director of Public Prosecutions has gone a long way towards improving the expert investigation of fraud by setting up fraud investigation groups within the Fraud Division. These groups are made up of lawyers and accountants who are available to assist and advise the police in all areas of a major fraud investigation right from the outset. This modern fraud investigation and prosecution department is capable of managing the investigation of even the most complex frauds. Those businessmen who are afraid that the police have not the ability to investigate complex fraud without their own thorough investigation to set the scene first can rest assured that the expert and highly-trained staff of this efficient department are available to give help and advice at all times.

The Department of Trade and Industry also has an investigation branch which was recently expanded by the appointment of an additional 190 staff who are now involved in the active investigation of many company law infringements, including fraud in business takeovers. Accountants and business advisers are also playing an increasing role in the investigation of fraud. Many firms of accountants offer their services in advising and training police officers and others, including their own staffs, in specialist areas of company law and fraud investigation. Much of their time may be given to the problems of fraud investigation and detection, and liaison between all these groups has increased considerably over the last few years. But not all the expansion is on the side of law and order, as the shock waves of the 'Big Bang' are still reverberating through the City. The argument for deregulation, when the City of

London was cut loose from its restrictions, was that it could bring spectacular growth. This may have proved to be so, but in every area of acceptable growth there is an element which is not so acceptable. In order to contain this problem the Stock Exchange has expanded its surveillance force, and has already had some success in the area of insider trading. It still remains to be seen how effective these measures will be, particularly in the area of international share dealing rings.

Just as the awareness of fraud and the interest in it shown by investigative agencies, by business management, by advisers and by academics has increased, so has the interest in the mass of surveys devoted entirely to the subject. These surveys often have common findings, many of them contained in the report by the *Fraud Trials Committee,* chaired by Lord Roskill (HMSO 1986). In their report they included not only recommendations on fraud trials but also recommendations on the investigation and prosecution of fraud. The Roskill Report advocated an increase in the resources available for fraud investigation, and stressed that this must be treated as a matter of urgency. It also suggested that a uniform system for investigating and prosecuting fraud should be established, instead of leaving this to fragmented government bodies and the police. It suggested that a new unified organisation could be achieved by developing the concept of the fraud investigation group which exists at present within the fraud investigation and prosecution section at the office of the Director of Public Prosecutions. Accountants are already employed in the fraud investigation groups and in some Fraud Squads, but the Roskill Report suggested that the role of accountants in fraud investigations should be recognised, and that all Fraud Squads should include a permanent accountant. The Committee recommended that as a first step towards achieving a unified system of detecting, investigating and prosecuting fraud, a Fraud Commission should be established which would have the following functions: and

(a) the supervision of the implementation of those of the Committee's proposals adopted by the government;

(b) the investigation of the efficiency with which fraud cases are conducted; and

(c)   the co-ordination between the various bodies which currently have responsibility for investigating fraud.

Once a serious fraud has been identified, a case controller should be appointed to spearhead its investigation and prosecution. He should be joined in his investigations by two prosecuting counsel, who would supply the necessary legal advice. This would relieve the Director of Public Prosecutions of the burden and at the same time answer criticism of its policy towards fraud cases.

The police should recognise the importance of the work of their own Fraud Squads and should provide a career structure within these Squads to encourage the development of the expertise necessary to deal with modern fraud. The police should also be given greater powers in their investigations of fraud, identical to those granted to the inspectors in the Companies Investigations branch of the Department of Trade and Industry.

The Roskill Committee suggested that all those involved in fraud cases should be given specialised training to ensure that the cases are handled competently and effectively. This would include not only investigators but also judges who, it is recommended, should receive regular tuition in accounting and information technology. Barristers should also receive some training in the technical matters with which they will have to deal, and some accountancy training should be included at pupillage stage. Post-qualification courses for barristers, similar to those required by solicitors, should also be included and such post-qualification courses should be taken into account by the prosecuting authorities in selecting a barrister to deal with a particular case. The Committee also recommended that police Fraud Squad officers should be given a much longer and more effective period of training. The recommendations of the Roskill Committee, the attitude of the business community, and the activities of all agencies involved in the investigation of fraud must be harnessed to unite in the fight against fraud. This is the only way that the present increase in the incidence of fraud will be contained and eventually reversed.